Bethle

Bethlehem Bound

Andrew Nunn

CANTERBURY
PRESS
Norwich

© Andrew Nunn 2022

First published in 2022 by the Canterbury Press Norwich
Editorial office
3rd Floor, Invicta House
108–114 Golden Lane
London EC1Y 0TG, UK
www.canterburypress.co.uk

Canterbury Press is an imprint of Hymns Ancient & Modern Ltd
(a registered charity)

Hymns Ancient & Modern® is a registered trademark of
Hymns Ancient & Modern Ltd
13A Hellesdon Park Road, Norwich,
Norfolk NR6 5DR, UK

All rights reserved. No part of this publication may be
reproduced, stored in a retrieval system, or transmitted,
in any form or by any means, electronic, mechanical,
photocopying or otherwise, without the prior permission of
the publisher, Canterbury Press.

The Author has asserted his right under the Copyright, Designs
and Patents Act 1988 to be identified as the Author of this Work

Scripture quotations are from the New Revised Standard Version
Bible: Anglicized Edition, copyright © 1989, 1995 National
Council of the Churches of Christ in the United States of America.
Used by permission. All rights reserved worldwide.

British Library Cataloguing in Publication data

A catalogue record for this book is available
from the British Library

ISBN 978-1-78622-448-4

Typeset by Regent Typesetting
Printed and bound in Great Britain by
CPI Group (UK) Ltd

Contents

Preface

You need to know two things about me to understand this book. The first is that I absolutely love Christmas. There is nothing really that I don't like about it, to be honest. The food suits me; I adore putting the decorations up; and singing carols non-stop, as I do in Southwark Cathedral, thrills my heart. But above all I love the accounts of the Nativity that we find in the Gospels of Matthew and Luke, and the contrast with St John's Gospel which takes centre stage as we get to Christmas Day itself. The accounts are full of little details and wonderful characters, and we know it all inside out. Except, I wonder if we do.

The second thing about Christmas that I really enjoy is imagining the back story to characters and situations in the scriptures. I suppose this is something of what St Ignatius of Loyola encourages us to do in the Spiritual Exercises. We need, I think, to get inside the story, discover the person, find ourselves there, in our imagination and in our praying.

Put these two loves together and the result is what you find in this book. We start from the point when Advent shifts a gear: that is on 17 December, the day the church calls O Sapientia. It seems an odd place to begin, but starting at that point enables us to become part of the final stage of the journey to Bethlehem and to what lies beyond it in the twelve days of Christmas.

Each day from 17 December onwards you will find the gospel reading for the Eucharist that day and a reflection on it. There is also a character to meet, someone I want to introduce you to. Most of the people you will know. Some of them are familiar characters from the Nativity; others are those we remember on the rich series of days that follow Christmas Day; others have never had a voice. The stories are of my own imagining, though I hope they pick up on what we do know from scripture and history. The book ends with a postscript on the final day of the Christmas Season, the Feast of Candlemas, the Presentation of Christ in the Temple. That chapter is written in a similar way to another book of mine, *The Hour is Come*, taking us through the day and its events in what I like to call 'real time'.

The whole book is interspersed with prayers. Some will be familiar as part of our heritage, but most of them are prayers I have written for this book which have sprung from my own reflections, my own imagining.

As Dean of Southwark I have had the privilege of accompanying many people on pilgrimage to the Holy Land. Pilgrims are always very excited on the day when we are Bethlehem bound, when the coach heads out of Jerusalem and through the entrance in the wall that separates Israel off from the Palestinian Authority. The journey to Bethlehem is now much more difficult, and Mary and Joseph would probably not be able to complete it today as they did then. That is a sobering thought as we pass by the Banksy murals on the forbidding wall. But it was a hard journey then and it is a hard journey now. However, whether we make it in fact or in our imagination, the journey is always life-changing, because at the heart of it is gift – the gift from God of God's own self in a baby laid in a manger.

Enjoy the journey. Thank you for travelling with me.

Andrew Nunn

Beginning the Journey

It's only 80 miles from Nazareth to Bethlehem, not that far really. In a good car you could do it in a couple of hours. But on a donkey, on foot, pregnant? They tell me it could take four days but even that, I think, would be pushing it. But that was the journey that Mary and Joseph made in order to respond to the command of the Roman occupying force that everyone return to their home town to be registered. They had no choice really. Compulsory registration would be a means of controlling the people, not of simply doing a census, counting who was there. Despite the circumstances, they had to go.

Many of us will be attending carol services in the lead-up to Christmas or in the days immediately after. Since it began in 1918, just after the end of the First World War, millions of people across the world have tuned in to hear the famous carol service from King's College Cambridge, the Festival of Nine Lessons and Carols. After the opening carol, 'Once in Royal David's City', with its wonderful solo verse, comes the Bidding Prayer written by Eric Milner-White in 1918 when he was Dean of Truro, which begins with these lines that provide an invitation to us:

> *Beloved in Christ, be it this Christmastide our care and delight to hear again the message of the angels, and in heart and mind to go even unto Bethlehem and see this thing which is come to pass, and the Babe lying in a manger.*[1]

Mary and Joseph made the journey, and we are invited to be Bethlehem bound with them. It is a kind of pilgrimage that we make, one that requires us, not to move physically from where we are but, as the Bidding Prayer describes it, 'in heart and mind to go even unto Bethlehem'.

I want to begin this journey – and I hope you will travel with me – from a particular point in Advent. Today, 17 December, marks a change in gear within our keeping of the season in that this is when we begin to use what are known as the 'O Antiphons'.

It is thought by some that as early as the sixth century a series of special antiphons were being used in the final days leading up to Christmas. An antiphon in Christian music and ritual is a kind of responsory sung by the choir or congregation, usually in the form of a Gregorian chant, to a psalm or other text in a service. These O Antiphons were written for use at Vespers (what we know as Evensong) before and after the Magnificat.

They are called the O Antiphons because each one begins with the vocative 'O' and follows it with a messianic description from scripture. They begin on 17 December, a day named as O Sapienta, with this text:

> O Wisdom, coming forth from the mouth of the
>   Most High,
> reaching from one end to the other,
> mightily and sweetly ordering all things:
> Come and teach us the way of prudence.[2]

But I don't want our journey to end when these antiphons end on Christmas Eve. The journey continues, because not only are Mary and Joseph Bethlehem bound – there are shepherds and wise men on the roads as well. So our journey will take us through to the Feast of the Epiphany, celebrated in both the eastern and western traditions of the church on 6 January, and beyond that to the very end of the Christmas Season, Candlemas, celebrated on 2 February.

Each day we will be meditating on the gospel reading set for the Eucharist. They will be familiar texts – but I hope that, just as in travelling through familiar landscapes we can end up seeing something new, so with this journey, that God will make himself known to us in the scriptures in new ways. We will also be meeting one of the characters from this Nativity journey because all of us are 'Bethlehem Bound'.

It is not an easy journey to make. That is brought out by T. S. Eliot in his wonderful poem 'Journey of the Magi'. Eliot takes as his inspiration a sermon by Bishop Lancelot Andrewes, former Bishop of Winchester, buried in Southwark Cathedral, who in his Christmas Day sermon preached before King James I at Whitehall in 1622 says something about the journey that Eliot then develops. Some lines from that sermon give us the memorable beginning to Eliot's poem, 'A cold coming we had of it', and to the journey we will make:

> *A cold coming they had of it at this time of the year, just the worst time of the year to take a journey, and specially a long journey. The ways deep, the weather sharp, the days short, the sun farthest off, in the very dead of winter.*[3]

What will our journey be like as we, with them, are Bethlehem bound? Who knows – it will be different for each of us. But one thing was the same for them all. At the end of the journey there was gift, and gift lies waiting for us as well. Jesus is God's gift of himself to us. Every other gift besides this pales into insignificance.

So pray with me please as we prepare to set off on the journey.

> Lord of the journey,
> with Mary and Joseph,
> with shepherds and wise men,
> I am Bethlehem Bound.
> Bring me with them
> to worship before Jesus
> baby, brother, Lord and Saviour
> and so make every journey
> a walk with you.
> Amen.

4

17 December

Matthew 1.1–17

An account of the genealogy of Jesus the Messiah, the son of David, the son of Abraham.

Abraham was the father of Isaac, and Isaac the father of Jacob, and Jacob the father of Judah and his brothers, and Judah the father of Perez and Zerah by Tamar, and Perez the father of Hezron, and Hezron the father of Aram, and Aram the father of Aminadab, and Aminadab the father of Nahshon, and Nahshon the father of Salmon, and Salmon the father of Boaz by Rahab, and Boaz the father of Obed by Ruth, and Obed the father of Jesse, and Jesse the father of King David.

And David was the father of Solomon by the wife of Uriah, and Solomon the father of Rehoboam, and Rehoboam the father of Abijah, and Abijah the father of Asaph, and Asaph the father of Jehoshaphat, and

Jehoshaphat the father of Joram, and Joram the father of Uzziah, and Uzziah the father of Jotham, and Jotham the father of Ahaz, and Ahaz the father of Hezekiah, and Hezekiah the father of Manasseh, and Manasseh the father of Amos, and Amos the father of Josiah, and Josiah the father of Jechoniah and his brothers, at the time of the deportation to Babylon.

And after the deportation to Babylon: Jechoniah was the father of Salathiel, and Salathiel the father of Zerubbabel, and Zerubbabel the father of Abiud, and Abiud the father of Eliakim, and Eliakim the father of Azor, and Azor the father of Zadok, and Zadok the father of Achim, and Achim the father of Eliud, and Eliud the father of Eleazar, and Eleazar the father of Matthan, and Matthan the father of Jacob, and Jacob the father of Joseph the husband of Mary, of whom Jesus was born, who is called the Messiah.

So all the generations from Abraham to David are fourteen generations; and from David to the deportation to Babylon, fourteen generations; and from the deportation to Babylon to the Messiah, fourteen generations.

I registered with a genealogy website. I had been watching those programmes where people trace their family, like *Who Do You Think You Are?* I wanted to know who I was, where I'd come from, what stock I was from. I knew a bit, of course. I had listened to both my grandmothers tell their own tales of family and houses, of distant memories and of people who had gone before them. I was under no illusion. I knew that I wasn't blue blooded or from wealthy landowners, I knew that I would be from more simple working folk. So it was really interesting when the information started to gather, when the clues came up, the digitalized records started to link and there was something of a family tree developing.

My paternal grandmother had always told me that the Nunns were originally cabinet makers from Ipswich; and, lo and behold, I found my way back to the eighteenth century, to Alfred Nunn and 'Nunn's Yard', where the workshop was and a maid and an apprentice were housed. My maternal grandmother had told me about a thatched cottage in a village called Kirby Muxloe in Leicestershire, and how in the past a 'Rainbow' married a 'Fairy'. And there it all was – a farm worker's cottage and a Mr Rainbow marrying a Miss Fairy.

Like pieces of a jigsaw it was coming together and making a bigger picture. And the roots – or is it the branches? – were being put in place, that complicated web which describes our lineage, who we are.

You will find in many great churches or cathedrals a Jesse Tree window. Jesse, the father of King David, lies at the base of the window and out of his side spouts a tree. On that tree, like fruit, are the characters that St Matthew puts in his genealogy of Jesus. The Jesse Tree is a visual representation of the gospel for today. The deacon or priest reading it at the Eucharist will have to make their way with care through all those names. It's a reading that we have only on this day: perhaps not a popular reading like the Beatitudes, but one given to us to root Jesus in the history of his people and to show the stock from which he comes.

In St John's Gospel Jesus speaks of himself as the vine. A couple of years ago I enjoyed a wonderful trip round the Champagne region of France and was fascinated as a viticulturist described the process of grafting on to old stock, stock that was resistant to disease, stock that would produce good shoots and great fruit, a bumper harvest. St Paul in his Letter to the Romans uses similar imagery, the stock and the graft. But in this gospel reading for today Jesus is described as springing from the one stock, the one root, that can trace its origin in Abraham, the father of the nation, the father of all nations.

St Luke also gives us a genealogy at the beginning of his Gospel – not right at the beginning as Matthew does, who wants to make his point immediately, but later on after the birth narrative. But what Luke does is to trace Jesus back to Adam, not Abraham. Luke in his inclusive, global, Gentile-embracing way wants to show that Jesus is from the root of 'Everyman' and not simply the root of the Jewish people. Matthew, however, writing for a non-Gentile audience, is happy to begin his route from root to fruit with the greatest patriarch.

As we take the Bethlehem road and become pilgrims together, Bethlehem bound as we begin these final days to Christmas, we are asked to consider who we are and where our story, our life journey begins. One answer will be as far back as records will take us, but your real story may begin elsewhere. Who are you?

> Creator God,
> you made me,
> you love me,
> you know me.
> May I know you
> and myself
> in your Son Jesus.
> Amen.

And now meet ... Jesse

Isaiah 11.1–3a

> *A shoot shall come out from the stock of Jesse,*
>   *and a branch shall grow out of his roots.*
> *The spirit of the Lord shall rest on him,*
>   *the spirit of wisdom and understanding,*
>   *the spirit of counsel and might,*
>   *the spirit of knowledge and the fear of the LORD.*
> *His delight shall be in the fear of the LORD.*

I laugh, to be honest, when I catch sight of myself in some grand window, the light shining through all that coloured glass, and me, lying there on my side, reclining like some rich potentate. If that's how you imagine me, well, you've got it wrong. I'm Jesse, the one you imagine having a tree growing out of his side – ridiculous. I wasn't rich at all – not poor, to be honest, but I never thought of myself as rich. I lived in a very little town, Bethlehem, and like many people in the town I was a shepherd. My flocks grazed on the wonderful hills that surround the town. When I stood at the door of my tent I could see them grazing away, content, as I was. People respected me because I had a lot of sheep and a lot of sons. They saw me as richly blessed. Eight sons in all, all of them good-looking lads, tall, dependable, even the youngest of them, David.

It isn't right for any parent to have favourites, but I don't mind telling you that David was the apple of my eye. His brothers had all grown up; David was a blessing in my old age. His eyes were bright, his face intelligent. He was as brave as any man and he walked around, well, with dignity. It's hard to describe. We were just ordinary, but he had the look, the bearing of a king. I was so proud to be his dad. I tried not to show it to the others. I didn't want the same thing to happen to them that happened to Jacob and his 12 sons, all that jealousy and rivalry between them. My lads were good and worked as a team.

I'd often send David out to them in the fields. As soon as he could walk I taught him to defend himself and the sheep. His mother made him a little bag to go over his shoulder and he would gather pebbles that he could use in his sling if he needed to. He was a fantastic shot and could scare off the lions and the wolves and the bears that you can come across in these hills.

I wish my own grandmother could have seen her great-grandson. Ruth would have loved him. They tell me she was a beauty in her day, a person of real spirit and courage, regal, an outsider who made her home in this town. People say that David reminds them of her, a shoot out of that stock. He must get what makes him special from somewhere.

You can imagine how surprised I was when one day a prophet came to town, Samuel, and asked to see my sons. No one could imagine why – they all had respect for me and my family, but we weren't anything special. He looked each one of them up and down. No; no; no; no; no; no; no. 'Have you any more sons?' asked the old man.

David was still in the fields and so we waited and very soon we heard the sound of him, whistling, singing, as he always did – did I forget to say he was musical? I called him to me: 'David, there is someone who wants to see you.'

'Yes,' said the old man, looking up to heaven. From his belt he took a horn of oil and poured it on the lad's head. David stood there, the oil running down over his robe, regal, just like a king.

'Once in royal David's city'. I have heard you singing that as I lay there in the window, a tree sprouting from me. You never know what your children will become.

> God of our ancestors,
> root me in good soil,
> that I may bring forth fruit,
> for today and tomorrow.
> Amen.

18 December

Matthew 1.18–24

Now the birth of Jesus the Messiah took place in this way. When his mother Mary had been engaged to Joseph, but before they lived together, she was found to be with child from the Holy Spirit. Her husband Joseph, being a righteous man and unwilling to expose her to public disgrace, planned to dismiss her quietly. But just when he had resolved to do this, an angel of the Lord appeared to him in a dream and said, 'Joseph, son of David, do not be afraid to take Mary as your wife, for the child conceived in her is from the Holy Spirit. She will bear a son, and you are to name him Jesus, for he will save his people from their sins.' All this took place to fulfil what had been spoken by the Lord through the prophet:

> *'Look, the virgin shall conceive and bear a son,*
> *and they shall name him Emmanuel',*

which means, 'God is with us.' When Joseph awoke from sleep, he did as the angel of the Lord commanded him; he took her as his wife.

He could have done it but in his heart he didn't want to. Just because she was pregnant didn't mean he loved her less. But he had to make a decision. Would he stay with her or let her go? It was a disaster in the making. Whatever he chose to do he would be wrong. If he let her go then what would her life be like – a young girl and a child, no man in the background? She'd be on the street trying to eke out an existence. Family and friends would want nothing to do with her, or her child. It was a terrible prospect. But if he let her stay, if she had her child and the child lived, he could end up the laughing stock. They were not fools, they would all talk. And he was old and she was young and they would know, and perhaps they would all end up having to leave.

In the musical *Joseph and the Amazing Technicolor Dreamcoat* there is a song with the chorus 'Poor, poor Joseph, what'cha gonna do?' It could have been written of another Joseph in another age. The dilemma that faced him was impossible. Heads he won, tails she lost. It was awful. And he was a good man, a righteous man, and she was a good woman, a righteous woman. Poor, poor Joseph.

His forbear, Joseph, sold into slavery, was a dreamer. His brothers hated him for it but in the end his dreams saved him and them. Joseph too was a dreamer. And in his dream an angel appears and tells him to do the radical thing, to have faith in God's purposes, to trust his better instincts, to do right by Mary and the child yet to be born. The angel didn't say that it would be easy, but the implication was that it would be right. Joseph had the confidence and the courage to listen, to take what the angel, what his dreams, told him and to respond in the right way.

The prophet Joel says:

> *I will pour out my spirit on all flesh;*
> *your sons and your daughters shall prophesy,*
> *your old men shall dream dreams,*
> *and your young men shall see visions.*
> (Joel 2.28)

It isn't wrong to dream, it isn't fanciful to have visions of what can be, it isn't pointless listening for the voice of the Lord. Jung was right when he said of dreams that 'they show the inner truth and reality of the patient as it really is: not as I conjecture it to be, and not as he would like it to be, but as it is'.[4]

Truth and reality – that is what was revealed to Joseph. He dreamt and when he awoke he acted and did what was right, and God was with him and God is with us. You are righteous, act righteously. As together we are Bethlehem bound, choose not the easiest path but the right path and if an angel speaks, listen.

> God, in the decisions I have to make today
> point me in the right direction
> and give me the courage, the clarity
> and the righteousness of Joseph.
> Amen.

And now meet ... Anne

Proverbs 31.28–29

> *Her children rise up and call her happy;*
> *her husband too, and he praises her:*
> *'Many women have done excellently,*
> *but you surpass them all.'*

My name is Anne. It's no use searching your Bible for me. I'm not there, don't even get a mention. Look in the Qur'an and you'll find me there. I'm described as highly spiritual, they call me Hannah and it says that I'm married to Imran, but others say that I'm married to Joachim. It's all very confusing.

The thing is that I was old. We'd wanted children but, well, it just never seemed to happen for us. I'd known a few women in our family that this happened to. It made some of them bitter, unhappy, as though they were unfulfilled. But, you know, I trusted God, that God knew best.

Then one day I was out. I'd been to the well to collect water. It was winter, the beginning of December, and so I was amazed at what I saw. There in a tree was a bird – not just a bird alone but one feeding its chick. This wasn't the season for chicks to be born but here it was. Something stirred inside me, a desire for a child that I'd never quite felt in this way before.

I went home with the filled water jar and said nothing to my husband but instead I prayed. You can read what then happened to me, not in the Bible as I said, but in something written by James, much later. He recorded the event like this:

> Behold, an angel of the Lord stood by, saying: 'Anna, Anna, the Lord hath heard thy prayer, and thou shalt conceive, and shalt bring forth; and thy seed shall be spoken of in all the world.' And Anna said: 'As the Lord my God liveth, if I beget either male or female, I will bring it as a gift to the Lord my God; and it shall minister to Him in holy things all the days of its life.'[5]

It was a few days later, 8 December, I remember it well. I knew – don't ask me how, it's a woman thing – I knew that I'd conceived, that a child, God's blessing, was growing in my womb. Over the weeks and months ahead I was proved right. My neighbours and friends were amazed – they'd written me off as 'barren'. How I hated that word, it made me sound like a useless piece of land whereas God knew that I was fruitful.

It was just as the intense heat of summer changed to the cooler days of September that the child was born. I'd meant what I said to that angel, that I didn't mind if it was a boy or a girl. When the midwife held up the screaming baby I saw that it was a girl – and she was a gift from God.

We named her Mary. She was an immaculate baby; she was a wonderful girl, and as I looked into her eyes as she grew it was like looking into eyes that saw heaven.

I don't really mind that no one plays me in a nativity play, that many people don't know my name. Some of us in life are in the wings, and that's OK – we can't all be centre stage. But I smile when I see little girls playing my beautiful Mary because the story couldn't have happened without me – and God.

> God of surprises,
> as you heard Anne's prayers
> and surpassed them in blessing
> so hear our prayers this Christmas
> and startle us with your goodness.
> Amen.

19 December

Luke 1.5–25

In the days of King Herod of Judea, there was a priest named Zechariah, who belonged to the priestly order of Abijah. His wife was a descendant of Aaron, and her name was Elizabeth. Both of them were righteous before God, living blamelessly according to all the commandments and regulations of the Lord. But they had no children, because Elizabeth was barren, and both were getting on in years.

Once when he was serving as priest before God and his section was on duty, he was chosen by lot, according to the custom of the priesthood, to enter the sanctuary of the Lord and offer incense. Now at the time of the incense-offering, the whole assembly of the people was praying outside. Then there appeared to him an angel of the Lord, standing at the right side of the altar of incense. When Zechariah saw him, he was terrified; and fear overwhelmed him. But the angel said to him, 'Do not be afraid, Zechariah, for your prayer has been heard. Your wife Elizabeth will bear you a son, and you will name him John. You will have joy and gladness, and many will rejoice at his birth, for he will be great in the sight of the Lord. He must never drink wine or strong drink; even before his birth he will be filled with the Holy Spirit. He will turn many of the people of Israel to the Lord their God. With the spirit and power of Elijah he will go before him, to turn the hearts of parents to their children, and the disobedient to the wisdom of the righteous, to make ready a people prepared for the Lord.' Zechariah said to the angel, 'How will I know that this is so? For I am an old man, and my wife is getting on in years.' The angel replied, 'I am Gabriel. I stand in the presence of God, and I have been sent to speak to you and to bring you this good news. But now, because you did not believe my words, which will be fulfilled in their time, you will become mute, unable to speak, until the day these things occur.'

Meanwhile, the people were waiting for Zechariah, and wondered at his delay in the sanctuary. When he did come out, he could not speak to them, and they realized that he had seen a vision in the sanctuary. He kept motioning to them and remained unable to speak. When his time of service was ended, he went to his home.

After those days his wife Elizabeth conceived, and for five months she remained in seclusion. She said, 'This is what the Lord has done for me when he looked favourably on me and took away the disgrace I have endured among my people.'

At certain times of the year shadows stretch a long way. It's to do with the angle of the sun, I suppose. Sometimes we look on the ground and our own shadow or the shadow of a tree stretches out before us. There is a shadow here that stretches from Abraham and his wife Sarah to Zechariah and Elizabeth. Both were loving, righteous couples, both were older and both desired children but didn't have any. To both an angel comes and makes a promise. Sarah thinks it is so ridiculous an idea that as she listens into the conversation of her husband with the angel she laughs from within the tent. Zechariah too is incredulous: he doesn't laugh but instead is struck dumb for his lack of belief.

The first miracle that Jesus will perform will be to change water into wine. He took what was unpromising, ordinary, not fruitful and transformed it – and the wine overflowed, more than they could ever need for a wedding reception. God does this trick, taking the least likely, the unpromising, the hopeless and transforming it. He takes the water and makes it wine, takes the barren and makes it bear fruit, places a baby in the arms of a couple who had given up hope, saying to an old man 'You will be father of many nations', saying to a priest at his duty 'Your wife will bear a son'.

My life isn't the best soil from which to produce fruit. I read the parable of the sower and see so much of myself there, in every aspect: the hard, compacted soil that won't give way, the shallow soil in which things can't take root, the overgrown ground in which a shoot would be choked, where stones and dryness abound. But out of the most unpromising soil God produces a harvest, out of water God makes wine, from the barren and the dry new life springs forth.

Sarah laughed and Zechariah was incredulous, and we laugh and are in awe at the wonder of God. There is no limit to what God can do. That is the truth, and when we stop believing it then we too will be dumb, as Zechariah was, only able to go through the motions in the sanctuary until his tongue was loosed and, with Sarah and with Elizabeth, he could laugh and praise the God of miracles.

As we are Bethlehem bound, let us look at the soil, look at the fields of our life and pray that we too will be fruitful.

> Make the barren soil of my life
> bring forth fruit,
> Lord of the harvest,
> Lord of my life.
> Amen.

And now meet ... Gabriel

Luke 1.19

> *The angel replied, 'I am Gabriel. I stand in the presence of God, and I have been sent to speak to you and to bring you this good news.'*

It's not a bad job really. Some of the other angels have a tougher time than I do. Take Michael – always fighting; take Raphael – always with sick people. But you see, I am Gabriel, and it's my job when there's a bit of good news to be shared to take it from God to whoever needs to hear it. I don't know why I got the job, but I'm not looking for another one.

But what surprises me, when I turn up, unannounced – that's the way we do it, we just appear – some people aren't as happy with good news as you'd imagine they would be. I went with a message to a priest: now you would have thought he would have been receptive to a messenger from God. And the thing was, it was something that he and his wife had been longing for for so many years. Everyone assumed that that was it as far as having a family was concerned. But I found him at his duties in the temple and surprised him with the news that his wife, Elizabeth, was to have a child. But instead of leaping for joy he questioned what I said to the extent that he was struck dumb until the child was born.

But it was different with Mary. I found her at her prayers. She was quiet, nothing more than a girl really, and I tried not to shock her. She listened, she asked a question and then she simply accepted what I'd said: 'Let it be with me according to your word.' And with that I left her. I made sure, of course, that I was there when the baby was born, but I wasn't alone, we all turned out, angels and archangels and the whole company of heaven. We filled the skies with a choir and we sang and sang and sang to God's glory.

> *Glory to God in the highest heaven,*
> *and on earth peace among those whom he favours!*
> (Luke 2.14)

Now I watch the children pretending to be me. All the little girls, and some of the boys, want to be angels, to have a halo, some tinsel, some wings, reminding people of what we did, what I did. I don't blame them – it's one of the best bits of the story. And I rejoice when I hear my own words repeated around the world as people pray.

> Hail Mary, full of grace.
> The Lord is with thee.
> Blessed art thou amongst women,
> and blessed is the fruit of thy womb, Jesus.
> Holy Mary, Mother of God,
> pray for us sinners,
> now and at the hour of our death.
> Amen.

20 December

Luke 1.26–38

In the sixth month the angel Gabriel was sent by God to a town in Galilee called Nazareth, to a virgin engaged to a man whose name was Joseph, of the house of David. The virgin's name was Mary. And he came to her and said, 'Greetings, favoured one! The Lord is with you.' But she was much perplexed by his words and pondered what sort of greeting this might be. The angel said to her, 'Do not be afraid, Mary, for you have found favour with God. And now, you will conceive in your womb and bear a son, and you will name him Jesus. He will be great, and will be called the Son of the Most High, and the Lord God will give to him the throne of his ancestor David. He will reign over the house of Jacob for ever, and of his kingdom there will be no end.' Mary said to the angel, 'How can this be, since I am a virgin?' The

angel said to her, 'The Holy Spirit will come upon you,
and the power of the Most High will overshadow you;
therefore the child to be born will be holy; he will be
called Son of God. And now, your relative Elizabeth in
her old age has also conceived a son; and this is the sixth
month for her who was said to be barren. For nothing
will be impossible with God.' Then Mary said, 'Here am
I, the servant of the Lord; let it be with me according to
your word.' Then the angel departed from her.

Charles Causley's poem 'Ballad of the Bread Man' begins
with Mary in the kitchen, baking a loaf of bread when
an angel flies in with a message: *'We've a job for you,' he*
said. The annunciation, the name given to this event, to
this announcing to Mary that she was to be the mother
of God's son, is one of the most depicted and celebrated
events in the Gospels. Walk around almost any art gallery
and you will find as many annunciations as you will find
crucifixions. The story of the young girl and the angel, of
that 'yes' that Mary in her innocence gives to God, has
captured the imagination of artists and poets and writers
and, of course, Christians in their worship in every generation. Causley's slightly irreverent take on it is just one
example and memorable for how he stages it.

My favourite depiction of the scene is in a painting that
can be found in the Philadelphia Museum of Art and is
by Henry Ossawa Tanner (1859–1937). He was the first
African-American painter to gain international acclaim
and the way he depicts the scene is, to me, stunning. One
writer commenting on Tanner's work says of this painting,
'"The Annunciation" (1898) expresses the intensity and
fire of religious moments, and the elation of transcendence
between the divine and humanity.'

But why should the annunciation and the crucifixion be such popular subjects for depiction in Christian art? Perhaps it is because, in both, God is announcing something life-changing to us, something we have responded to in every generation. When God through the angel Gabriel announces to Mary that she will be the mother of his son it is the incarnation that is being announced, that 'God so loved the world that he gave his only Son' (John 3.16). On the cross something else is announced, the message of salvation: God loves us so much that not only will he take flesh in Jesus and live as one of us, but in his flesh and for that same love God will die for us.

Mary was stunned at the message she received, and we remain stunned with her – so stunned that we have to keep revisiting the news of incarnation and the news of salvation to make sure we have the message fixed in our minds. And the message? It boils down to three words – 'I love you.' Those simple words keep us journeying.

> God of love
> in the womb of Mary you found a dwelling place,
> on the cross you claimed crown and throne;
> may I trust in your love
> revealed in crib and cross.
> Amen.[6]

And now meet ... Mary

Revelation 12.1–2

> *A great portent appeared in heaven: a woman clothed with the sun, with the moon under her feet, and on her head a crown of twelve stars. She was pregnant and was crying out in birth pangs, in the agony of giving birth.*

My name is Mary. You will think that you know me well. You will have seen me in so many places, looking down at you, from a window, from a screen, a picture, a statue. You may have lit a candle before me, asked me to pray for you, cried before me, thought that I was the only one you could talk to. You may have travelled long distances to a place that I was supposed to have visited, appeared in. You may have been in a shrine at which I was the centre of attention; looked to me for your healing, appealed to me for clemency. It's so strange. You think you know me so well, but I bet you would pass me in the street if our paths could cross, not recognizing me at all. In fact, I hardly recognize myself.

I'd lived a quiet life. Having older parents meant that I had to help around the house even earlier than other girls around me in Nazareth did. My mother was finding it hard to fetch the water each day from the well – so that quickly became my job, and the sweeping and the cleaning and then the preparation of the food, the baking of the bread.

I would have liked to have played with the other girls, but I didn't have time with all this other stuff I had to do.

It would be untrue to say that I didn't resent it at times. Don't misunderstand me, I loved my parents, but I'd have loved to have let my hair down, just for a moment. Even though I'd never really been to many, I knew that I loved a party, a wedding, with the wine flowing and the guests awaiting the bridegroom and the women tending the lamps and the young women waiting to escort the bride.

But my life seemed to be shaped to my being like a hand-maid, a servant. When I wasn't cooking and cleaning I was quiet, I said my prayers, I waited.

It had been an ordinary day when my ordinary life became extraordinary. The chores were done, my parents had gone to market, I was alone in the house, thinking. And then, he was there, speaking to me, a messenger from God. I was scared at first, moved close to the wall where I was sitting as if I could get away. But any fear passed quickly, for the messenger brought peace into the room and into my heart.

And what I was told made me thrill to the core of my being. I was to be a mother, of a very special baby. 'How?' I asked. I had been betrothed to a local carpenter my father knew, Joseph, but we'd hardly seen each other and never spent time alone together yet.

'The Holy Spirit', was the answer. It was to be a holy baby, God's baby.

My reaction? Well, I surprised myself. 'I'm God's hand-maid,' I said. It was what I was used to. I had done it for my parents, I would do it for God, I would do it for the child who was, as I spoke, being planted deep inside me.

That was almost nine months ago and those have been turbulent months. When it became obvious to anyone who cared to look at me my mother stopped me going to the well. I'd tried going at midday when only those women went who were shunned by the community. But she wanted to spare me that shame, and so sent me off to a cousin down south who was also expecting a child.

And then, when I returned home, so that my mother could be my midwife, we were all told that there was to be a count of all the people in the country by the Romans. As I was now about to be married to Joseph (who had been wonderful about all this baby business – my father had chosen so well, a true husband for me) we had to pack our bags and head off to his home city of Bethlehem. I could hardly contemplate the journey – but I had no choice. And that is where I am now, on the back of a donkey, heading from Galilee to Judea.

You think you know me so well, but am I more plaster than flesh for you, object of fantasy and fascination, rather than real? I am a real girl caught up in extraordinary happenings. When one of your little girls is dressed up in blue and white and walks in, pretending to be me, she's more like me than the statue that you look at. She's prob- ably really nervous, trying to remember her lines, a little bit of stage fright, not wanting to drop the baby. That was me, the quiet girl at the well, chosen for the purposes of God, a handmaid, not a queen.

> Mary, pray for us.
> In your humility and simplicity
> you reveal so much of God.
> May my life be lived more humbly
> and simply.
> Amen.

21 December

Luke 1.39–45

In those days Mary set out and went with haste to a Judean town in the hill country, where she entered the house of Zechariah and greeted Elizabeth. When Elizabeth heard Mary's greeting, the child leapt in her womb. And Elizabeth was filled with the Holy Spirit and exclaimed with a loud cry, 'Blessed are you among women, and blessed is the fruit of your womb. And why has this happened to me, that the mother of my Lord comes to me? For as soon as I heard the sound of your greeting, the child in my womb leapt for joy. And blessed is she who believed that there would be a fulfilment of what was spoken to her by the Lord.'

Waiting at an arrival point is fascinating. Whether it's an airport or a railway station or anywhere where a rendez-vous has been arranged, it is just wonderful to watch people arrive and meet. At St Pancras Station in London it is celebrated in a monumental statue of a couple kissing. She is swept up into his arms with the sheer delight at meeting. And as you watch you notice the moment of recognition, the flash of joy, the beaming smiles, the tears of joy that all go before the embrace. However long they have been apart, now they are together and even the onlooker is moved with joy.

The traditional site of the visitation of Mary and Elizabeth is just outside modern Jerusalem in the hill country. Leaving the city you descend through wooded hills into a valley where the village of Ein Karem is located. It is here that Elizabeth and Zechariah lived – just near enough for him to walk to the temple to fulfil his duties but far enough out, in this temperate valley, to provide a good home for this aged couple.

Mary was, of course, living in Nazareth but she decides to make the journey from Galilee to Judea to see her kinswoman. As part of the message that she received from Gabriel about her own pregnancy, her miraculous pregnancy, she was told that her kinswoman Elizabeth, beyond the usual age of childbearing, was herself pregnant. Miracles were abounding and Mary, needing support, goes to the only other person who might understand a little of what she is going through.

It could not have been an easy journey for her to make, but she did it and she arrived. When the two women saw each other their tears, their laughter, their joy must have been unbounded.

The psalmist in Psalm 85.10 writes:

> *Steadfast love and faithfulness will meet;*
>   *righteousness and peace will kiss each other.*

But there is another meeting taking place, for the joy of the mothers is paralleled by the joy of the babies in their mothers' wombs. The women embrace and the unborn John leaps for joy recognizing the presence of Jesus for the first time. And the mothers? They felt their joy deep within them. It must have been heart stopping.

John would, many years later, point to Jesus. John is baptizing by the Jordan when Jesus comes to him in the crowds to be baptized and John, pointing, says, 'Here is the Lamb of God.' John points to Jesus, identifies him, recognizes and focuses our attention on the one for whom he and we are waiting.

In da Vinci's cartoon of the Virgin and St John in the National Gallery in London, John is looking at Jesus with great intensity. His attention directs ours. He spent his life pointing to Jesus. And it is the vocation of every Christian to look for Christ: to point away from self to the one who comes to save us, the one for whom we are Bethlehem bound.

Lord, may my life be a pointer to Jesus,
may my heart be filled with joy
at every meeting with you.
Amen.

And now meet ... Joseph

Matthew 1.16

Jacob the father of Joseph the husband of Mary, of whom Jesus was born, who is called the Messiah.

Things weren't too bad actually. I know that when we were having a drink we would complain about the Romans – 'What have they ever done for us?' – but in fact they'd brought a lot of work to our region. There was a huge amount of redevelopment going on and that meant more money around. If you were good at your trade – and they knew what they wanted – then there was work to be done, and if you proved yourself reliable and not a troublemaker then you were almost guaranteed work. Not far away from where I lived was the city of Sepphoris. That was the place where my fiancée, Mary, and her parents originated, though they live not far from me in Nazareth now. But since that city was ransacked it's being completely rebuilt, the jewel of Galilee, and I'm part of the crew.

Sorry, I should have said, I'm Joseph. If I told you that I was part of the family of King David, that I can trace my line right back to him, you wouldn't believe me. The work-worn hands, the dishevelled look of the working man might make you think that I was pulling your leg. But I'm not – it's true.

33

I've mentioned that I'm betrothed. It took quite a while to find a wife. Work was taking me away, I had plenty to do, but the years were moving on and I did want a family while I was young enough to enjoy it. I knew this old fellow, Joachim. As I say, he and his wife Anne came from Sepphoris, and I was in the market one day selling a few things I'd made and this old-timer came up and started chatting. When I told him that I was working on the big construction site we became even friendlier – you know how it is with men.

So one thing led to another; I went to theirs for a few meals, all served by their daughter. She was quiet, she was beautiful. I only saw her when she brought the food in, she never looked at me. But she had an air – well, it's hard to describe. With some women beauty is on the outside but with her it seemed to be who she is, simply beautiful. I spoke to her father about her. No plans had been made for her marriage and when I said that I would be honoured if he would consider me I was amazed that I wasn't sent home with a flea in my ear!

That was some months ago. Plans are in hand for the marriage. All was going well. I say 'was' because something unforeseen happened. I was absolutely exhausted. The journeys backwards and forwards to work take their toll, I'm not cut out for commuting! So I'd been fast asleep and all of a sudden I was awake, as awake as you are at midday, and the room was filled with light.

It was startling but not frightening. A messenger had arrived – from God. I say it as though it's an ordinary occurrence; of course it isn't, but when it was happening it didn't feel so weird. But what he told me was.

It seems that innocent, beautiful Mary is pregnant! Time stopped for an instant. My world collapsed. What was this joker saying? Mary, who never went out really; Mary, the handmaid? All the options ran through my mind. But before I could say much I was told, 'Do not be afraid to take Mary as your wife.'

To hear she was pregnant was a shock, to be told the child was God's child was a bigger shock. But just as Mary brought peace with her, so did this messenger. I accepted the words, I accepted God's will.

At the moment we're not in Nazareth, but on our way to Bethlehem, Mary and me. You remember me saying about King David. Well, the Romans want a proper census taken so we've all had to head home to our ancestral roots. For me that's back to the home of David and his father, Jesse, who I think you have met. Thousands of people like us are on the move, north and south, east and west, and we're just a few days away from the goal of our journey. Mary is on the donkey, I'm walking beside her. My feet are as sore as my hands usually are. I don't know where we're going to stay when we arrive, I don't know what'll happen about the baby. I'm meant to be the breadwinner and the protector of my family and at the moment I feel as lost and unsure as dear Mary must be feeling.

I'm trusting, trusting God. When this story is told I bet many a lad will want to play me. Just as long as they show me as solid and dependable, I don't care what they wear; just as long as they show me as willing to do God's work, I'm happy.

God,
may I use my hands,
my feet, my mind,
my whole being,
to work for you,
whatever that work is.
Amen.

22 December

Luke 1.46–56

> And Mary said,
>   'My soul magnifies the Lord,
>   and my spirit rejoices in God my Saviour,
>   for he has looked with favour on the lowliness of
>   his servant.
>   Surely, from now on all generations will call
>   me blessed;
>   for the Mighty One has done great things for me,
>   and holy is his name.
>   His mercy is for those who fear him
>   from generation to generation.
>   He has shown strength with his arm;
>   he has scattered the proud in the thoughts of
>   their hearts.

He has brought down the powerful from
their thrones,
and lifted up the lowly;
he has filled the hungry with good things,
and sent the rich away empty.
He has helped his servant Israel,
in remembrance of his mercy,
according to the promise he made to our ancestors,
to Abraham and to his descendants for ever.'

And Mary remained with her for about three months
and then returned to her home.

I adore musicals, in fact I wouldn't mind living in one! For
me it is one of the joys of Christmas television, the chance
to see *White Christmas* again, or *The Sound of Music*
or any of those great Rogers and Hammerstein movies.
There are two archetypal scenes for me that typify what
a musical is all about (although the opening scene of the
first Austin Powers movie comes a very close third): they
are Gene Kelly singing in the rain and, of course, Julie
Andrews in the opening sequence of *The Sound of Music*
running through that alpine meadow.

Both scenes express for me sheer joy and the desire that
exists within us to express that joy by dancing and singing. It's like David dancing before the Ark as it enters
into Jerusalem (2 Samuel 6). It is like the man cured by
the apostles at the Beautiful Gate of the temple, 'walking
and leaping and praising God' (Acts 3.8). They couldn't
restrain their joy, they had to express it, they felt as if they
would burst if they didn't.

The gospel today is the very familiar text of the Magnificat. In response to the joy that Mary feels as she meets Elizabeth, in response to the joy that Elizabeth's unborn child expresses in his mother's womb, Mary sings this song. In fact this is the first of three 'songs' that St Luke includes in the birth narrative. Mary, Zechariah and Simeon are all given songs to sing.

The truth is of course that Luke doesn't say they burst into song. It is the church that has taken these texts and used them as 'canticles' – the word literally means 'little song' – and along with psalmody has built around them the Offices, the times of prayer, that form the golden thread that runs through each day. It is the Magnificat, the Song of Mary, that is at the heart of Evening Prayer, Evensong, Vespers, whatever name we choose.

Joy Cowley has written a modern free translation of Mary's song which captures something of its mood:

My soul sings in gratitude.
I'm dancing in the mystery of God.
The light of the Holy One is within me
and I am blessed, so truly blessed.[7]

St Ambrose, one of the great Doctors of the Church, in his commentary on the Magnificat writes:

In the heart of each one may Mary praise the Lord, in each may the spirit of Mary rejoice in the Lord.[8]

While we journey to Bethlehem, while we are Bethlehem bound, it is good to sing, it helps the journey. But be careful what you sing.

Mary's words are familiar to us, but they are deeply radical. This is no sweet song but the voice of revolution, a song of new justice, a song in which the overturning of society is described. This is subversive stuff, but as Mary sang it she sang as the prophet of a new order which her son would herald, for he would be king of a new kind of kingdom and of that kingdom we are citizens. The truth is that the musical into which we are drawn is like no other; and the kingdom that we await as we journey to Bethlehem is like no other; and this young girl who sings with the voice of the kingdom is a matchless maiden like no other. So we dare to pray with St Ambrose:

> In my heart may Mary praise the Lord.
> In my life may the spirit of Mary rejoice.
> Amen.

And now meet ... the Donkey

Zechariah 9.9

> *Rejoice greatly, O daughter Zion!*
>   *Shout aloud, O daughter Jerusalem!*
> *Lo, your king comes to you;*
>   *triumphant and victorious is he,*
> *humble and riding on a donkey.*

You know, I wish I'd been born a horse. I used to say to my mum, 'Mum, I wish I'd been born a horse.' And she used to say to me, 'Shut up making such a racket, you're a donkey!' Where I grew up, there were some horses. They were kept in a field close by. I used to watch them – long legs, strong body, proud head. And when their owner came, well, he was a soldier – long legs, strong body, proud head. They were suited to each other. He jumped on to that horse's back and they rode off and all you could see was dust. I watched while my Master loaded more wood on to my back.

That was my job, you see. My Master was a carpenter, and he was working on this building site in a place called Sepphoris. Every time he had a job to do, beams for a ceiling, lintels for a door, frames for a window, the wood was loaded on to me, and I had to trudge alongside him to where the wood was needed.

While he was working I had a chance to talk to some of the other donkeys. Some of them had a terrible time, beaten, ill fed, left without water in the heat. Some were skin and bones, some had scars. I was lucky: my Master was lovely. He treated me well and fed me well – that's why I'm a bit on the broad side, but as I said to a friend, more space to load the wood on to!

I heard them saying that to ride a horse shows your high status, if you ride a donkey it shows your humility. You see, that's why I want to be a horse, to be proud, not a symbol of humility, not an object of ridicule and fun.

That's how it felt until a few days ago. The day began with nothing to suggest that it was going to be different from any other day. And then from the house there seemed to be a lot of activity. A young woman and an older couple arrived. My Master was busy getting things together, but not the normal load of wood. Then he came out and flung some bags across me, some skins of water, some skins of wine, I could smell some fresh baked bread. And then the girl appeared. She was wrapped up because it was winter, it was cold, and in the hills you could feel that it might just snow.

My Master came and helped her on to my back. You know, she was as light as a feather. Perhaps it was because I was used to being loaded with wood, I'd grown familiar to a heavy load. But this burden was easy, this burden was light.

The older couple waited while we set off. We headed south and I just walked. I didn't know where I was going but my Master knew and he led me while the young woman sat there. They talked but their voices were gentle. I could almost hear an echo of some singing as I went – it must have been wind in the olive trees, but it was as though from somewhere I could hear children singing something about a little donkey, as though they knew me.

Since then we've been walking, my Master and me, and Mary – that's the girl's name – has been sitting there, carefully, gently on my back. She's having a baby, I've heard them talking about that. So I'm carrying not one but two people. It's not just she who is riding on my back but the baby as well. And I'm proud – don't ask me why, but I feel as honoured as one of those grand horses, as important as one of those who pull a grand chariot, as though I too carry a king.

Perhaps the baby won't need to ride a donkey again, or maybe the baby will – who knows?

I see some children playing by the roadside, pretending to be me – one at the front, another at the back, a pretend donkey. They laugh and I laugh with them. Life is good.

> Lord, help me not to want to be who I'm not
> but to be fully the person
> you created me to be.
> Amen.

23 December

Luke 1.57–66

Now the time came for Elizabeth to give birth, and she bore a son. Her neighbours and relatives heard that the Lord had shown his great mercy to her, and they rejoiced with her.

On the eighth day they came to circumcise the child, and they were going to name him Zechariah after his father. But his mother said, 'No; he is to be called John.' They said to her, 'None of your relatives has this name.' Then they began motioning to his father to find out what name he wanted to give him. He asked for a writing-

tablet and wrote, 'His name is John.' And all of them were amazed. Immediately his mouth was opened and his tongue freed, and he began to speak, praising God. Fear came over all their neighbours, and all these things were talked about throughout the entire hill country of Judea. All who heard them pondered them and said, 'What then will this child become?' For, indeed, the hand of the Lord was with him.

There are so many people who are agonized by the name their parents gave them. But it is their name and for better or worse that is the name they are known by. I can remember some people at school being very unwilling to disclose what their middle name was. Perhaps it was because they were named after a grandfather, an aunt, given some name that every member of the family had had for 'generations'. I began by saying that I had found records of an Alfred Nunn working as a cabinet maker in Ipswich in the eighteenth century. Well, he was in a long line of Alfreds, or should I say my paternal grandfather was. They were all Alfred! Fortunately the pattern was broken when my father was born and was called Peter, and fortunately for me it was his Christian name that became my middle name. I am very pleased with Andrew Peter to take me through life – I feel as though I got a good deal out of it.

There was consternation among the neighbours and relatives of Zechariah and Elizabeth. The eighth day had arrived, the naming day for a newborn child, and the neighbours were eager to know the name because that would mean so much. The assumption was that the first-born male child would take his father's name. But his father had been struck dumb because he didn't believe the word of the angel. So it was his mother who had to name him. 'He is to be called John,' she says in a very firm way.

There was no argument and when they sought confirm-ation from his dumbstruck father they had an even more emphatic response: 'His name is John.'

It was a great name to choose. The Hebrew *Yochanan* means 'Yahweh is gracious', 'The Lord is gracious'. It is what the parents of the child had experienced, the graciousness of the Lord, who had given them what they could hardly dream of. It was a gift beyond any gift and they wanted to remember this always. Every time they looked at their child, every time they called his name they would remember the graciousness of God.

Remembering that God is gracious and that we should be gracious as well is part of our response to what God has done for us. The former Chief Rabbi, Jonathan Sacks, wrote:

> *In thinking about religion and society in the 21st century, we should broaden the conversation about faith from doctrinal debates to the larger question of how it might inspire us to strengthen the bonds of belonging that redeem us from our solitude, helping us to construct together a gracious and generous social order.*[9]

To create a gracious and generous social order, a commu-nity in which the true goodness of God is reflected, nations which deserve the name of the good society – that is the calling that we have received, all people of faith, working with people of good will.

Gracious God,
may I bear your name,
may I bear your nature,
just and righteous one,
Amen.

And now meet ... the Innkeeper

Hebrews 13.2

Do not neglect to show hospitality to strangers, for by doing that some have entertained angels without knowing it.

To be perfectly honest, business had not been good. You see, my wife and I found that we had some spare space once the children had grown up, got married and left home. My wife was a great cook and, well, I like to think of myself as a generous host. I was getting a bit slower – age you know – so the farming I used to do wasn't as easy. So we decided just to keep a few animals in the stable beneath our living space and take in guests, become an inn. It's hard changing jobs, learning new skills, from being a farmer to an innkeeper. But that's what I now am, an innkeeper.

As I say, business hasn't been so good. So I can't say that I was unhappy when those Romans under the Governor Quirinius decided to have a snap registration of all the citizens of the country. Nor was I unhappy when they said that everyone had to go to their hometown to be registered. You see, Bethlehem is my hometown, so my wife and I don't have to move, unlike some of our neighbours. But I've heard that plenty of people are on the move and they'll be looking for somewhere to stay. Perfect!

So we've been spending the last few weeks since the announcement cleaning the old place and getting it ready to receive guests. My wife got into every corner, even found a coin she'd lost in one of the darker recesses of a room. She swept those floors as if in doing so she kept the law!

My job was beneath, where the few animals are. I changed the straw, cleaned out that old manger, got rid of a bit of the junk that my wife says all men accumulate in 'their space'. We're not expecting to use it, but with it being under the house my wife wanted it to smell sweeter than it often does.

The animals watched me, gently chewing, wondering, I suppose what I was up to.

Finally, we went to the market and got some more provisions: grain – the barley round here is the best in the country and it makes great bread; well, you know that that's what this city is named after – Bethlehem, 'House of Bread'; and some oil so that doesn't run out; wine of course; and some herbs and vegetables.

After we'd stored it all, we stood back and looked at our handiwork. 'Fit for a king!' my wife said.

I laughed. 'We won't find any king staying in this old place.'

'Well, you know whoever comes will be a special person to me,' she replied. She is a wonderful woman, always so ready to help, even when it seems impossible to me.

That was all a few days ago and since then things have become a bit manic. Be careful what you pray for, someone once told me – God just might answer your prayers! There's been a constant stream of people entering the city, looking for a place to stay. We're almost full and people are still arriving. My wife's running around the place in order to look after them, a neighbour's girl has come in to help and I'm trying to make sure the animals they arrived with are OK. Donkeys mainly, so I've put them in a pen round the back. They're not going in the stable, noisy creatures – we wouldn't get a wink of sleep.

You know, we were stood outside the front of the house last night. My wife was wiping her hands on her apron and we were just getting a breath of the cold fresh air. The night sky was beautiful. Then my wife pointed. 'I haven't seen that star before,' she said. And it was new and large and you could fool yourself into thinking it was getting closer. We went back inside. We'll see what tomorrow brings.

> Lord,
> may my home be prepared to receive you,
> may my heart be ready to embrace you.
> Amen.

24 December

Luke 1.67–79

Then his father Zechariah was filled with the Holy Spirit and spoke this prophecy:

'Blessed be the Lord God of Israel,
   for he has looked favourably on his people and
      redeemed them.
He has raised up a mighty saviour for us
   in the house of his servant David,
as he spoke through the mouth of his holy prophets
      from of old,
   that we would be saved from our enemies and
      from the hand of all who hate us.

Thus he has shown the mercy promised to our
    ancestors,
  and has remembered his holy covenant,
the oath that he swore to our ancestor Abraham,
    to grant us that we, being rescued from the hands
      of our enemies,
might serve him without fear, in holiness and
    righteousness
  before him all our days.
And you, child, will be called the prophet of the
    Most High;
    for you will go before the Lord to prepare his ways,
to give knowledge of salvation to his people
  by the forgiveness of their sins.
By the tender mercy of our God,
    the dawn from on high will break upon us,
to give light to those who sit in darkness and in the
    shadow of death,
    to guide our feet into the way of peace.'

He had been unable to speak, for over nine months. When he doubted the word of the angel who came to him in the temple to tell him that his wife, even though she was beyond the age of childbearing, would have a son, he was struck dumb. It was only on the eighth day after the birth of the child, when he was named, that Zechariah got his voice back. He wasn't lost for words.

This is the second 'song' that St Luke gives us in the opening chapters of his Gospel. Luke says that Zechariah spoke this prophecy, but in turn the church has sung it as the Benedictus, every morning as part of Morning Prayer or Matins. Like Mary's 'Magnificat' it is a wonderful song, all-embracing, full of celebration, full of prophecy.

John the Baptist, often called the last of the Old Testament prophets, the bridge between the old and the new, the one who straddles the false divide in our Bibles, is the son of a prophet. Rather than denying God's promises and losing his voice, Zechariah affirms and celebrates God's promises and finds his voice.

The French aristocrat, writer and aviator Antoine de Saint-Exupéry, in his book *Night Flight*, says:

In every crowd are certain persons who seem just like the rest, yet they bear amazing messages.[10]

Perhaps to their neighbours Zechariah and Elizabeth seemed like any elderly couple, a familiar part of the village landscape. Then extraordinary things begin to happen to them and in the end they bear 'amazing messages'. They seemed just like the rest – and in many ways they were – but both, in the end, allowed themselves to be the agents of prophecy, Elizabeth in her womb, Zechariah on his tongue.

We have to ask if the age of prophecy is dead or whether we just don't hear prophecy in the same way any more – and what is prophecy anyway? We can easily get it confused with predicting the future, and of course there is an element of that in it. But it is much more, I think, about speaking God's truth into the situations in which we find ourselves. Often this is described as 'speaking truth to power' and in many ways that is what the child John grew up to do. Another way in which this calling is often described is 'disturbing the comfortable and comforting the disturbed'. It may sound slick and clever as a description, yet that is an essential part of what it means to have 'a prophet's tongue'.

In fact prophecy is much more central to the vocation of the church than we sometimes give it credit for. We can imagine it to be a peripheral activity which has really died out, and so some words of the philosopher Jean-Paul Sartre are salutary:

All men are prophets or else God does not exist.[11]

Sartre sees prophecy as that important.

> Lord,
> give me the courage of the prophet
> to speak truth to power
> and the wisdom to know
> when that is needed.
> Amen.

And now meet ... the Shepherd

1 Samuel 16.11

Samuel said to Jesse, 'Are all your sons here?' And he said, 'There remains yet the youngest, but he is keeping the sheep.'

You get a lot of time to think, doing this job. They don't like you going to sleep, but they can't stop you thinking. All my family have been shepherds, so it was natural that I'd become one too – a shepherd. You begin just following the other men, seeing how they do it, learning to use a sling shot if a wild animal approaches and threatens the sheep. You have to learn how to move the sheep and the goats on, to find new pasture. You have to learn how to get them into a pen, into a fold. You have to know when they're not well and you have to be able to count so that you know if one has gone astray. And when you're learning, sometimes you'll be sent off, if they can spare you, to find the sheep that's lost and bring it back. But apart from that, you just sit there – and think.

The other thing you can do, thinking about it, is learn how to play an instrument. Some of us have learned how to play the pipe, and if you'll excuse me if I say this, I'm not bad at it.

The thing we don't do often is go into town. You see, down there, to be perfectly honest, we're not very popular. We have a bit of a reputation for being rough and coarse and smelly, for liking a fight and for swearing. Obviously I'm being polite talking to you but normally when I'm talking to the others – well, let's say I wouldn't talk like that in front of my mother!

You're wondering what the prospects are? Well, I suppose I could be in charge of a gang of shepherds, working for some wealthy owner, but apart from that, not a lot. Except that what I do keep at the back of my mind is that King David started off doing what I'm doing. He came from these parts, probably walked these same hills with the sheep he looked after. It was the harp with him, not the pipes, and he was a great thinker, a great poet, making up those songs:

> *The LORD is my shepherd; I shall not want.*
> *He maketh me to lie down in green pastures: he leadeth*
>   *me beside the still waters.*
> (Psalm 23, KJV)

I can imagine him out here, writing that down. So you see, we're not quite what those townies think of us. We can be full of surprises, though I admit we are a bit smelly and no one in their right mind would invite us into their home before we've had a good wash!

The nights seem so long at this time of the year. I often sit on my own, not too far from the fire, but where I can get a bit of space and a bit of silence. And over the last few nights I've been watching the stars. You get to know them, the constellations, quite well when you're out here as often as I am – Orion, the Pleiades. But over the last few nights there's been something different, a star I hadn't seen before. I'm used to comets, shooting stars that sweep across the sky. But this one is different. It seems to be getting nearer but very steadily, and it seems to be heading to where we are. The others say I think too much, that it's gone to my head, that I should have another drink and forget it. But I'm intrigued.

So I'm looking forward to tonight when the sun sets and the stars appear to see what the sky will hold. But that's for later. Now I need to see where those sheep have got to.

> Lord,
> may I watch for the signs of your coming,
> may I be alert to you around me,
> may I be ready to welcome you into my life.
> Amen.

24 December

11.00pm

Luke 1.78–79

> *'By the tender mercy of our God,*
> *the dawn from on high will break upon us,*
> *to give light to those who sit in darkness and in the*
> *shadow of death,*
> *to guide our feet into the way of peace.'*

Within those prophetic words of Zechariah, spoken as his tongue was freed and John was named, are these verses. They speak of the dawn, and we are approaching midnight. Tonight, in the heart of the darkness, a light will burn from within a stable. That light will be Christ. He is the light that will banish the darkness and give hope to those 'in the shadow of death', for in his light we see life and in his life we see light.

In these last minutes before Christmas Day we wait for that light to be kindled, for that light to come into the world. We wait with the whole of creation, in the silence; we wait with the whole of creation, in the dark; we wait with Mary and Joseph; we wait for love to come among us; we wait for Christ to illuminate our lives.

> God our Father,
> in this night you have made known to us again
> the coming of our Lord Jesus Christ:
> confirm our faith and fix our eyes on him
> until the day dawns
> and Christ the Morning Star rises in our hearts.
> To him be glory both now and for ever.
> Amen.

And now meet ... the Star

Ecclesiasticus 43.9

*The glory of the stars is the beauty of heaven,
a glittering array in the heights of the Lord.*

I am very quiet. I just shine. That's what stars do, they shine. We've been around a long time, from the fourth day of creation, when God made us 'to give light upon the earth'. So that is what I do, what we have always done, shine with light for the world. Normally, though, I'm on a fixed path: I move as I have done for all time, across the sky. People who look up know where I am, know where to find me. They plan their journey by looking for me, fix their place by finding me. My light can be counted on.

Then I was asked to move, sent on a journey, sent Bethlehem bound, a sign, a shining light in a dark sky. So I abandoned my place among the other stars and they twinkled their goodbyes as I went on a mission.

You will often see a child in a nativity play acting as me. They will be dressed top to toe in tinsel, everything will be sparkling, and perhaps on a pole someone will have made a star just like me, but covered in foil with some flashing lights and easy enough for the child to carry.

Mine is a non-speaking part in the whole story. But you don't always have to make a noise to make a difference.

Silent night, holy night!
All is calm, all is bright.[12]

The children sing and I move and then stop, 'over the place where the child was'. I shone as brightly as I could. That is what I do, I shine; I give light upon the earth. But you know what? I have always shone so brightly that people could find me wherever they are. But there was one shining brighter than me that night, one who was also silent, the child I was leading people to. They say that he is 'the light of the world', that our creator God placed the son as the brightest star that all could follow. I was now reflecting his light into the darkness of the world.

Jesus, true light,
shine with your divine brightness
that all darkness may be defeated
and that I may reflect your light
into the world.
Amen.

25 December

John 1.1–14

> *In the beginning was the Word, and the Word was with God, and the Word was God. He was in the beginning with God. All things came into being through him, and without him not one thing came into being. What has come into being in him was life, and the life was the light of all people. The light shines in the darkness, and the darkness did not overcome it.*

> *There was a man sent from God, whose name was John. He came as a witness to testify to the light, so that all might believe through him. He himself was not the light, but he came to testify to the light. The true light, which enlightens everyone, was coming into the world.*

He was in the world, and the world came into being through him; yet the world did not know him. He came to what was his own, and his own people did not accept him. But to all who received him, who believed in his name, he gave power to become children of God, who were born, not of blood or of the will of the flesh or of the will of man, but of God.

And the Word became flesh and lived among us, and we have seen his glory, the glory as of a father's only son, full of grace and truth.

I suspect that there can be a measure of disappointment when people come to church on Christmas morning for Communion and hear this gospel reading. What? No shepherds, no angels! What? No Mary, no Joseph! What? No baby Jesus, no ox, no ass! Instead of the readings that paint the traditional picture of Christmas – and they come only from Matthew and Luke's gospels – we are given the beginning of John's Gospel with undoubted beautiful language ('especially in the King James Version, Vicar') but with dense theology. For people who like a bit of magic and sparkle at Christmas this gospel just doesn't do it.

And yet it is the most wonderful piece of scripture and the most powerful attempt to describe what is at the heart of all that we are celebrating. The details of the Nativity are wonderful, the star and the stable, the manger and the angels, the shepherds and the wise men, and we couldn't have a performance of the Nativity by the Sunday school without them. But they can't do any justice to what it is that we are really celebrating: that is the incarnation, and it requires us to engage in serious reflection.

But perhaps you say that today is not the day for serious theological engagement and exploration of such a doctrine. There are sprouts to cook and a turkey to roast, a pudding to boil and pies to be baked. We want to open our presents, we want to watch the Queen, we want to chat to family (or avoid them), we want to get our feet up and head down and sleep off the lunch. Maybe tomorrow we can think about the incarnation – let's just settle for Bethlehem today, for that is where we have been bound.

Yet it is precisely into Bethlehem and wherever we are that God is made incarnate; into the midst of the busyness and distractions of the day that the child is born; into our lack of time and inability to give our attention that a baby cries and his mother looks with love into the eyes of God's son. That is the wonder and the reality of the incarnation. John tries, with the limitations of words, to describe what has happened in the deepest way possible:

And the Word became flesh and lived among us.
(John 1.14)

Jesus enters the hustle and bustle of an overflowing town, with people rushing here and there. No one really noticed, just some outsiders, who came into the town at the prompting of angels. They weren't welcome in town, smelly, unruly, loud-mouthed shepherds – but they were the only callers at the stable that day, the only ones to kneel at the manger, the only ones to bring anything with them.

Most people today will be rushing past the stable door, to get to Mum's, to get things done, to be with friends. But the truth remains and is as powerful as it has ever been:

And the Word became flesh and lived among us.

Sir John Betjeman's most famous Christmas poem is called simply 'Christmas', and the ending remains as powerful today as when it was first written. With the constant question 'And is it true?' the poem reaches a conclusion that takes us to the heart of the mystery of the incarnation and the sacramental life of the church: 'God was man in Palestine and lives today in Bread and Wine.'

Yes, it will still be true tomorrow. God is with us, and we have seen his glory. And it will be true every day for you and me that, as we say in the creed:

For us and for our salvation
he came down from heaven:
by the power of the Holy Spirit
he became incarnate from the Virgin Mary,
and was made man.[13]

It is true and it will be true even for those who will always walk past the stable door, bound for somewhere else. But we are here, for we have been Bethlehem bound.

Lord Jesus Christ,
your birth at Bethlehem
draws us to kneel in wonder at heaven touching earth:
accept our heartfelt praise
as we worship you,
our Saviour and our eternal God.
Amen.

And now meet ... the Cast

Luke 2.6–7

> While they were there, the time came for her to deliver
> her child. And she gave birth to her firstborn son and
> wrapped him in bands of cloth, and laid him in a manger,
> because there was no place for them in the inn.

Jesse says:
Something strange is happening in my branches. It feels
like spring though it is midwinter. I'm like a fig tree bearing fruit in the wrong season. But all my branches feel
alive, stirring, as though fresh life is running through
them. What is happening?

Anne says:
I've tried to busy myself around the house and Joachim
keeps telling me they'll be all right. But I can't stop thinking about my Mary, so far away, all on her own. I know
she has Joseph with her, but this is a time for a girl to be
with her mother and with the other women. We know
what to do. But what does he know, he's a carpenter not
a physician and so many things can go wrong. I wonder
where they are. I wonder if she's OK. I wonder if the
baby's been born. I wonder ...

Gabriel says:

I've never heard such singing. We all turned out, angels and archangels and all the company of heaven. Those poor shepherds. Scared out of their wits at first but there was one who listened and made the others come back and hear what we had to say and what we sang. Who'd have thought that such tough men could be so frightened by a group of singing angels! But as I told you before we have this habit of just, well, being there, unannounced. And we were so full of joy – a new king, a new baby, peace on earth, good will among all people. There was so much to sing about.

Mary says:

It feels like I'm in a dream. The journey was awful. I thought it would be difficult but in fact it was worse than I could imagine. I'd assumed that after making the same journey a few months ago, there and back to see Elizabeth, it would be the same. But it wasn't. It was colder, the road seemed harder and I knew that at any moment my baby could be born. But Joseph was so lovely. Being together like this has meant that we've had the chance to really get to know each other. What a gentle man. What a kind man. I've been blessing God that my father found me such a husband. He kept on saying, 'Just around the corner, just over the next hill, we can almost see it.' In the end we laughed every time he said something like that – but you know, that made the journey that little bit easier.

And when we finally saw Bethlehem – well, we both almost cried. But neither of us had imagined what we'd find when we walked into the town. The place was full of people and as we went up and down every street, at every place there was a sign saying, 'Full', 'No room'.

I kept asking, 'What are we going to do?' But Joseph kept saying, 'The Lord will provide.' And the Lord did provide.

To be honest I wasn't bothered in the end where we stayed – I just needed to be able to lie down. And within a short time the baby came and I held him in my arms – and wept for joy. It feels like a dream, but this is real, and God is with us.

Joseph says:
I think it was the worst journey I'd ever made. You know that I was backwards and forwards from Nazareth to Sepphoris so it's not that I'm unused to travelling, but this was so much worse than any daily commute! For a start it's a long way, and it was getting colder, and Mary was so uncomfortable. But I did what I could to encourage her.

What a nightmare when we arrived! I hadn't really thought about that bit, and anyway what could I have done? But with everyone on the move and us arriving quite late at night every inn was full. Mary looked exhausted as she sat on the back of the donkey. I knocked on each door just to get the same response: 'Full.' 'Full.' 'Full.'

'But look at my wife,' I said. 'She's going to have a baby.'

'Full.'

It felt as though it was the last chance, the final door. 'The Lord will provide,' I said to her. The innkeeper came to the door. I could see his wife behind him, shaking her head but looking concerned. 'Full,' he said. Then he looked at us. 'But there is the stable beneath the house. I cleaned it out and it's fresh and you can use that if you want. It's not great but ...'

'The Lord bless you and keep you,' I said. He took a light and showed us in. 'Is it OK if we bring our donkey in as well?'

'Well ... OK,' he said.

Then he was gone. Mary lay down. I was unpacking what the donkey had been carrying. And then I heard her – Mary cried out and I ran to her. The baby was coming. I had no idea what to do. This all happened away from men, the women looked after it. 'Hang on,' I said and ran to the top of the house. Although she'd shaken her head, I knew the innkeeper's wife was kind. 'Please,' I said. 'My wife. We need you.'

She grabbed a pot of water off the fire and some cloth and followed me. Like those great women at the birth of Moses, Shiphrah and Puah, she helped the baby to emerge into that dark night. Mary gasped, the baby cried. 'It's a boy,' cried the innkeeper's wife. 'Congratulations!' But we knew it was a boy. The angel had told us.

The Donkey says:

The last few miles were the worst and Mary seemed to get heavier and heavier. But I took it gently and slowly and my Master was kind. When we arrived at Bethlehem we went from house to house and that seemed to make me more tired than the journey.

At last he found somewhere – and somewhere we could be together. It'd been the three of us for so long, night and day, and I wanted to stay with them and not be put with some Judean donkeys I knew nothing of (they're not like Galilean donkeys – much more trouble). But as luck would have it we ended up in a stable and so, of course, I could stay. Someone had put fresh straw down and there was hay. There was an old ox in the corner, but he just sat there, chewing away, as they do, nothing to say, but that's oxen for you.

I drank some water and ate something and then my Master ran out and ran back with a strange woman and everything seemed to be happening. Then a baby cried, and I looked up and the ox looked up and we saw Jesus. We saw Jesus.

The Innkeeper says:
I told you how busy it was getting – well, it got worse. Everywhere there were people, a knock came at the door all the time. 'Tell them we're full,' said my wife. And so I did. It was late and we were getting ready for bed. The guests were all back, some had rolled in after having a drink and they were snoring away. Just some water to boil so that it would be sweet for the morning and then we could turn in.

Another knock. 'Not now, not so late,' said my wife. 'Get rid of them.'

I opened the door. There was a man with a very young girl. She was on the back of a donkey. All three of them looked exhausted. 'Please,' said the man.

'We're full,' I said. Then I looked at them and all of a sudden I thought of that story of Abraham and Sarah entertaining those three angels. I know one of this group was a donkey, but that was such a story of hospitality. 'We have a stable,' I said.

The man looked delighted. So I took them into it and though I hadn't let any other donkeys in I led in all three of them. 'That'll be fine,' said the man. The girl said nothing. So I left them.

It wasn't much later when there was another bang on the door. 'What now?' said my wife.

It was the man. 'Please,' he said. 'My wife. We need you.' My wife grabbed a few things and ran down. I kept out of the way.

When she came back she said it was a boy. Mother and baby were doing well. But she was surprised that they weren't surprised it was a boy. Strange. We went to sleep.

The Shepherd says:
I'd been thinking, looking and thinking. I'd been watching that star I told you about. The other guys said I was imagining it, that all that thinking was playing tricks with my head. But I'd swear on the Holy Scriptures that it had come nearer, that it was now overhead.

But I was brought back to earth with a bump when suddenly, where there'd just been stars, the whole sky became alive with light and the silence was broken by what sounded like the most amazing singing. And it wasn't just me, the others saw and heard it as well. I'm ashamed to tell you that my first reaction was to run. We were all terrified, but something kept us there and that was when we heard it, that a baby had been born, the Saviour, the Messiah, the Lord. They said it was good news; I thought it was great news.

As quickly as they'd appeared, the sky was back to normal except for that one big star which now seemed to light up the whole countryside. 'What are we waiting for?' said the chief shepherd. 'Let's go and see if what we've heard is true.' He grabbed his stick, I grabbed my pipes, another grabbed a lamb (well, even shepherds don't go visiting without a gift) and we ran down the hill.

To be honest I didn't quite know what to expect. When we found the place, and it wasn't hard because the star was illuminating the spot, we went in. It was a stable, like the stables every home had. There was nothing grand at all about it, just a stable, and what we found there was just a baby – like my little brother when he was born.

Except ... it's made me think. It was ordinary and it was extraordinary. I felt a kind of peace in that place that's indescribable. We all felt it, and we all knelt, there in the straw. What a sight we must have been: the young girl, the older man, a donkey and an ox, the innkeeper and his wife who'd heard us arrive – and there in the middle, the centre of attention, the baby. What a scene, what a night, what a nativity.

The Star says:
I shine as brightly as I can, so that shepherds can see the wonder, so that others can find their way, so that light falls upon the earth even in the darkest night.

And ... and Jesus says nothing but is the Word that God speaks to the waiting world.

> Lord Jesus Christ,
> your birth at Bethlehem
> draws us to kneel in wonder at heaven touching earth:
> accept our heartfelt praise
> as we worship you,
> our Saviour and our eternal God.
> Amen.

26 December

Matthew 10.17–22

*Jesus said, 'Beware of them, for they will hand you over
to councils and flog you in their synagogues; and you
will be dragged before governors and kings because
of me, as a testimony to them and the Gentiles. When
they hand you over, do not worry about how you are to
speak or what you are to say; for what you are to say
will be given to you at that time; for it is not you who
speak, but the Spirit of your Father speaking through
you. Brother will betray brother to death, and a father
his child, and children will rise against parents and have*

them put to death; and you will be hated by all because of my name. But the one who endures to the end will be saved.'

Boxing Day was traditionally the day when servants and tradesmen received gifts from their employers. With delight and some anticipation they would open their 'Christmas box' to see how generous their overlord was. I hope you got what you wanted when you opened your presents yesterday. There is something wonderful about looking at all those gifts under the tree, their contents hidden from us by cardboard and wrapping paper. As children we would attempt a sneaky feel, a shake to see if we could identify what awaited us, my sister on the lookout for our parents, me having a quick examination of what lay there, waiting for us, waiting for Christmas Day.

They are of course nothing in comparison with the real gift of Christmas, the child lying in the manger, the one for whose birth we have been Bethlehem bound. In the poem 'Christmas' by John Betjeman, from which I quoted yesterday, the comparison is made between the gifts we give and the gift God gives, between the 'bath salts' and 'hideous tie' and the fact that 'God was man in Palestine'. We need reminding.

But Boxing Day holds a surprise. We might imagine that we would spend the day thinking more about what had happened the day before in that Bethlehem stable. We could reflect a little more on those others who, like us, were Bethlehem bound – angels and shepherds, and others still on the road. But no. Instead, today in the calendar of the church is the Feast of St Stephen, the first martyr of the church.

In his play *Murder in the Cathedral* T. S. Eliot picks up on this fact in the sermon that Archbishop Thomas Becket preaches as the interlude in the action of the play. The Archbishop is preaching in Canterbury Cathedral on Christmas morning 1170. He reflects on the fact that the feast day of the first martyr of the church follows immediately on our celebration of the birth of the Saviour. His own martyrdom is of course not far off as he says these words.

It was hard to know what had been wrapped up for us in those gifts under the tree, and it was only by taking off the wrappings that we were able to find out. Was it something we wanted, or something we didn't? Was it something we had hoped for or not? Was it expected or a surprise?

We have seen many babies; and looking into the crib with Mary and Joseph we see another baby, crying, needing to be fed, wanting to be held. Just a baby. But we need to look deeper. The force of Becket's sermon in the play is that you can't separate Christ's birth from his death, that the two go together.

Taking the child from the crib into our arms has consequences. The gift of the child to the world is free – Christ is a gift to the world, freely given for love, just as grace is that unearned free gift of God in our lives. But loving the gift has consequences.

One of the horrors of recent years has been the increase in the number of brutal attacks on Christians in the Middle East by radical Islamist forces. At one point, we heard how the initial Arabic letter for Nasrani, the name given to Christians in those countries, was painted on the homes of Christians so that they could be identified for slaughter, for martyrdom. I heard of one family, all together in their home, killed by a group of IS soldiers. And why? Because they dared to hold the gift to themselves, the Christ child, dared to be known as followers of Jesus. Like St Stephen they paid with their lives for the one who came to bring us life.

The story of St Stephen's martyrdom is in the Acts of the Apostles, not the Gospels. You can read it in Acts 7.54–60. But the full story can be read in the whole of Acts 6 and 7. It is worth reading for the amazing and courageous speech that Stephen makes before the council. But just before the speech begins, as the members of the council were looking at Stephen it says this:

> *And all who sat in the council looked intently at him, and they saw that his face was like the face of an angel.* (Acts 6.15)

Bethlehem was surrounded by angels bringing the message of Good News, that the Saviour had been born. There were still angels sharing that same Good News in Jerusalem; and there are still angels doing it now – and with their lives.

Loving God,
as I accept your gift,
as I hold the Christ
may I be ready to be a witness
to the one who gives us life.
Amen.

And now meet ... Stephen

My grandmother used to grab hold of me when I was little. She would squeeze my face between her hands and kiss me. 'He has the face of an angel,' she would say to my mother, and then squeeze and kiss me again. I didn't really know what she was talking about but I didn't mind the attention. My grandmother was kind. I used to follow her round as she took fresh bread to her neighbours, the old ones, the lame ones, who could no longer bake for themselves. I clung to her skirts as the old ladies and the old men cooed over me – 'Such a good boy you have.'

It's hard to think of those days without weeping. I am Stephen and I am speaking to you from prison. The cell I'm in is dark and smelly, I feel the damp wrapping itself around me, not the fond embrace of my grandmother any longer, but the cold cling of death. I hear the rats even though I can't see them. 'How did a good boy end up in prison?' I hear you asking. Well, it may sound ridiculous but I was taking bread and good news to the people of the city. I was doing what I learned from my grandmother – except it is more than that.

I was in the temple and saw a crowd in the colonnade where the teachers gather, so I made my way over to find out what was going on. There was a group of men there, northerners by their accents, who were talking excitedly about a man called Jesus. It wasn't the first time I'd heard his name. Around Passover he'd been the talk of the city and ended up being executed by the Romans. Then there were some unbelievable stories circulating that he'd come back from the dead. I dismissed it all then. But now, hearing what these men said, well, it made a difference. My heart was strangely warmed, I felt excited. So when the crowd dispersed I went up to them. It was James who spoke to me, he seemed to be a bit of a leader among them.

To cut a long story short they invited me to a meal that evening and I went. From that moment on I was one of them, a follower of the man Jesus, who I'd never met but who'd changed my life. Then James said that they needed help. There was so much for the Twelve (that's what he called them) to do that they needed people to take bread around. I could do that, I knew how to do that. It seemed that Jesus had passed bread around and said it was his body. The Twelve wanted people to be fed with good bread and good news. In fact they chose seven of us to go and be servants, *diakonos*. It was an honour, the crowning of my life. In fact my name, Stephen, means 'crown'. It was an honour, a crown, to take the bread, and break, and share it.

And that is why I'm here, in chains. Waiting. In fact I can hear footsteps outside, a key in the lock. They have come for me. Holy angels, stand by me.

> Jesus, servant king,
> may I serve the needs of others
> whatever the cost might be.
> Amen.

27 December

John 21.19b–25

Jesus said to Peter, 'Follow me.' Peter turned and saw the disciple whom Jesus loved following them; he was the one who had reclined next to Jesus at the supper and had said, 'Lord, who is it that is going to betray you?' When Peter saw him, he said to Jesus, 'Lord, what about him?' Jesus said to him, 'If it is my will that he remain until I come, what is that to you? Follow me!' So the rumour spread in the community that this disciple would not die. Yet Jesus did not say to him that he would not die, but 'If it is my will that he remain until I come, what is that to you?'

This is the disciple who is testifying to these things and has written them, and we know that his testimony is true. But there are also many other things that Jesus did; if every one of them were written down, I suppose that the world itself could not contain the books that would be written.

Yesterday we left Bethlehem for a moment and looked at the first martyr, Stephen. Today we are still not in the stable, the place where we have been bound, but are with John. This is John, Apostle and Evangelist, the one who is depicted in the Gospels as a young man, who reclined next to Jesus at the Last Supper, who was there with Peter and James at all the significant moments in the gospel. This is the John whom we associate with the Fourth Gospel which surprised us on Christmas Day, and with the Letters and the book of Revelation. This is John who didn't die a martyr's death as did the other apostles but lived out his days in enforced exile on the island of Patmos. (Or did he die in Ephesus? We don't really know.)

That is the tradition and it has long been the case that he is celebrated on this day within the octave, the eight days of the initial Christmas celebration.

John is often known as John the Divine. This title pays tribute to him as the first great theologian of the Christian church. It is the use of the word 'Divine' that we also find when we are talking of such groups as the 'Caroline Divines' or the 'Anglican Divines', people like Lancelot Andrewes, John Cosin, Thomas Ken, Richard Hooker and Jeremy Taylor.

But there is something intriguing which I find in the gospel reading for this feast day, and it is that hint at more. Even after the excesses of Christmas Day and Boxing Day there is probably still more lined up for us. The image of little Oliver standing with his bowl in the workhouse and saying 'Please, sir, I want some more' is one that stays with us. We want more. And this is what John seems to promise, or at least to suggest: that there is more to be had, that there are untold stories of Jesus and so many to be told:

> *If every one of them were written down, I suppose that the world itself could not contain the books that would be written.* (John 21.25)

It is a tantalizing verse. We want to know, we want more, we want to know all that Jesus did. This is not the only place in which John makes mention that there is more. At the end of the previous chapter it says:

> *Now Jesus did many other signs in the presence of his disciples, which are not written in this book. But these are written so that you may come to believe that Jesus is the Messiah, the Son of God, and that through believing you may have life in his name.* (John 20.30–31)

This is the real truth of the matter. Of course, more could be said about Jesus. Everyone who experienced him could have told their own story, every community he touched had their tale to tell. The books are still being written and the encounters are still being had: I can write about my experience of Jesus and you can write of yours and we could fill the world and the Web and social media with our words. There is more; but John is saying to us that what we have been given is enough. It is enough to know that the child in the manger 'is the Messiah, the Son of God'. This is all we need to know, this is all we need to believe.

We have been on a journey to Bethlehem, Bethlehem bound. But life, Christian life, is all about journey. It is all about pilgrimage and there is a destination, and one that is not so different from the destination of this journey. The destination is Christ, knowing Jesus, being one with him as he is one with us. Professor Alister McGrath writes this of the journey:

> *It encourages us to think ahead, and look forward with anticipation to the joy of arrival. One day we shall finally be with God, and see our Lord face to face!*[14]

This is what John helps us to do, to see the Lord face to face and to know him as the promised of God, the Word made flesh; John is the 'Divine' who leads us to the divine and to find in that divinity our own true selves. For John tells us that Jesus said:

> *I came that they may have life, and have it abundantly.* (John 10.10)

It is that abundant life that we find as we look into the crib and adore God in human form.

Merciful Lord,
cast your bright beams of light upon the Church:
that, being enlightened by the teaching
of your blessed apostle and evangelist Saint John,
we may so walk in the light of your truth
that we may at last attain to the light of everlasting life;
through Jesus Christ your incarnate Son our Lord.
Amen.[15]

And now meet ... John

These days I spend a long time looking out at the sea, in fact I have a lot of time to do it. This sea, though, is quite different from the one I used to know, the one we said was the shape of David's harp, Kinneret, the Sea of Galilee. Now I know that it wasn't a sea at all – you never lost sight of land – but then we thought it was a sea. As I look out from this island all I can see is the sea. And it was by the sea that I first met him.

My name is John. I was with my brother James and two others: Simon, who everyone called Peter because he was built like a rock, and his brother Andrew. We were fishing; that was our job. I was much younger than the others but my mother Salome and my father Zebedee wanted me to learn the family trade. To be honest I'd have preferred to be studying, reading. I loved picking up books left by those who travelled through where we lived on the Via Maris. They came from all over the region but especially from Greece and Rome. I tried to pick up what knowledge I could, but what I had to learn was how to get a big catch out of the waters.

Then Jesus walked into my life and I ended up walking into his. Everyone said he had a soft spot for me. All I knew was that when we were eating he wanted me at his side and when anything big was happening he wanted me there. He was like an older brother. There was something of the love of a father for a son about him, and the love of a brother for a brother. What I do know was that he taught me about love.

Don't get me wrong. My parents loved us, but Mum was a bit pushy, a bit ambitious, wanting to push us forward, embarrassing us in front of the others. Dad was tied up in the fishing business, sometimes almost literally with all those nets to mend. They loved me, but not how he loved me.

In the end they killed him, the one who really loved me. They nailed him to a cross and hung him there to die. The older guys ran away. I stayed, with Mary, Jesus' mother. She was like a mum to me, even though my own mum was there as well, following to the end. Then we buried him.

It should have been the end of the story, but it wasn't. When the Sabbath was over we went to the tomb and it was empty. Mary Magdalene claimed to have seen him, said she had talked to him, told us he had called her by name. I didn't really believe her until it happened to me.

We were back by the sea, where it all began. It was first light, we had caught nothing. Then we saw the figure of a man on the beach, heard him calling to us. In the end we realized it was Jesus. He fed us, then took Peter to one side. Then the strangest thing happened. Unusually, I was hanging back. Peter turned round and said to Jesus, looking at me, 'Lord, what about him?'

And Jesus said to him, 'If it is my will that he remain until I come, what is that to you?' So, I am waiting, by this sea, thinking, dreaming and writing. All those books I managed to get sight of – well, something remained in my memory. I learned to write – and so I write about him, and about how he taught me to love. I'll go on writing, until, well, until the waiting is over and I see him again.

> God of love,
> may I tell the story
> of my love for you,
> of your love for me.
> Amen.

28 December

Matthew 2.13–18

After the wise men had left, an angel of the Lord appeared to Joseph in a dream and said, 'Get up, take the child and his mother, and flee to Egypt, and remain there until I tell you; for Herod is about to search for the child, to destroy him.' Then Joseph got up, took the child and his mother by night, and went to Egypt, and remained there until the death of Herod. This was to fulfil what had been spoken by the Lord through the prophet, 'Out of Egypt I have called my son.'

When Herod saw that he had been tricked by the wise men, he was infuriated, and he sent and killed all the children in and around Bethlehem who were two years *old or under, according to the time that he had learned from the wise men. Then was fulfilled what had been spoken through the prophet Jeremiah:*

'A voice was heard in Ramah,
  wailing and loud lamentation,
Rachel weeping for her children;
  she refused to be consoled, because they are
    no more.'

We are back in Bethlehem, but we would rather not be here. Time has moved on. Others have been Bethlehem bound, three visitors from the east. They saw a sign in the heavens that alerted them to the fact that a new king had been born, and so they came to pay him homage. But in their desire to do just that, to find the child, they alerted the one who was already seated on an earthly throne to what had happened.

Herod's paranoia was triggered. There was no way some baby was going to take his throne. And so he comes up with a solution.

One of the most disturbing facts of life is how often it is the most innocent who end up paying the price, bearing the burden, suffering the pain. The ones least able to help themselves become the victims of the brutality and the mania of others. This year that we are about to leave behind, like most years, will have seen more than enough examples.

History is littered with the bodies of the innocent. In antiquity it is the legendary tale of the rape of the Sabine women, supposedly around 750 BC, which captured popular imagination. The Roman men were seeking wives from their neighbours who were suspicious of the rise of Rome. So, unable to get wives willing to come, they took them by force. The term 'rape' in this context means something more like abduction. But the story provided rich material for Renaissance painters, and in their work we see all the force of the attack on the innocent.

It is a story that reminds us that in war and tribal rivalries it is the women and children who bear so much of the abuse and pain. In modern wars sexual violence is a weapon used in a frightening way. Women, not necessarily killed, but left scarred, injured for the whole of their life. Girls carrying the baby of their attacker, hating what is in their wombs – and children looking on as their mother is raped.

Herod launches his attack on the children of Bethlehem, all because he is desperate to protect his power, viciously hungry to retain what he has, paranoid that this baby will take it away from him. This feast day, Holy Innocents Day, following so quickly on Christmas, once again serves to make us sit up and take notice. 'Weren't we just hearing angels singing of the peace this child would bring – but what am I seeing here?' we may ask ourselves.

> 'Do not think that I have come to bring peace to the earth; I have not come to bring peace, but a sword.
> For I have come to set a man against his father,
> and a daughter against her mother,
> and a daughter-in-law against her mother-in-law;
> and one's foes will be members of one's own
> household.' (Matthew 10.34–36)

Jesus' words to his disciples later in his ministry are fore-shadowed in the events we remember today. And they are hard words for us to come to terms with. In that city where peace came in the form of a child a sword was drawn to slaughter all the innocents.

The greatest theological dilemma for religious people, Christians among them, is why bad things happen to good people. It is that question and the inability to get a good answer that makes many people give up on God. It is even more the case when evil is done in the name of religion, when it is the religious people who have the drawn sword and blood on their hands.

I wish I had an answer for you, for myself. My only answer is that the incarnation means that God shares in our pain and does not simply look on it from afar. That doesn't stop the bad things happening – well, not immediately – but ultimately it will. That may be unsatisfying but it is all I can offer.

There are three Herods in the story of Jesus – Herod the Great, the one we are thinking about today, Archelaus who succeeded his father, and Herod Antipas before whom Jesus would stand in the hours before his crucifix-ion. Herod was in fact the family name, and the story of this family would be bound up for ever with the story of Jesus: their fear of losing their power would cause them to kill the innocents, behead John the Baptist and tacitly agree to the killing of Jesus, God's own son. It is a story that we have seen and, I fear, will continue to see played out by numerous despotic regimes around the world.

And as it happens we will hear the cry of Rachel echoing through the centuries, the cry of the mother weeping for her children, the cry of the innocent. And perhaps our only response is to cry with them.

> Into your hands, Lord,
> we commend all the innocent
> who have suffered at the hands of tyrants.
> Make us restless to see better days come
> when the peace you bring
> will be the peace we live.
> Amen.

And now meet ... the Children

We used to watch our brothers and sisters play, out in the streets, our playground. We were too young to play; some of us hadn't even learned to walk, let alone run. So we watched them and laughed with them. We couldn't wait to be as big as them, to run with them, to laugh with them.

Then our mothers would come back from the well, fresh water in their jars, collecting us on their way home. Sometimes though we went with them, strapped to their backs, rocked and shaken as they walked over the rough paths that led from our houses to the well. Our mothers talked, we listened. Some of us couldn't yet talk. Some could say 'Abba' for father, some could say 'Immah' for mother. But we all knew that the best way to get their attention was not with words but by crying. Cry long enough and they would stop and give you what you wanted.

Our mothers loved coming to the well because this was where Rachel came. She was a mother here a long, long time ago. But our mothers still talked about her, in fact they would go to where she was buried, on the edge of the town, and leave a stone to show they had been and had said a prayer. I heard them say that they often thought they could hear the echo of Rachel's singing, of her laughter as they moved about the town, doing their daily chores.

One day there was a new mother among them. She had a very tiny baby in her arms, much younger than we were, not long born. She would come to get water but she would often sit on the edge of the well and feed her baby and talk to the others. She wasn't from here, but her husband's family were. They had come down for the census and she'd had her baby and so was living here for a while until they were all ready to make the long journey back to where they lived. Our mothers loved her and would carry her water back to where they were living, so she could carry her precious son, Jesus.

Then, one night, it happened. It was past bedtime; our fathers had extinguished the last light and we had all lain down to sleep when there was such a noise. There was the sound of women screaming, the sound of children crying, the sound of men shouting, the sound of horse's hooves and doors being crashed open.

We were ripped from the arms of our mothers, all of us, my friends and I, ripped away – and then ... nothing.

It isn't the sound of Rachel's singing that echoes round the streets of our town any longer, it's the sound of her weeping. We had all lost our innocence that night, as we, the innocent, were taken.

> Lord Jesus,
> Child of Bethlehem,
> hold to yourself all the innocent,
> all the victims,
> all who weep
> and look for peace.
> Amen.

29 December

Matthew 10.28–33

Jesus said, 'Do not fear those who kill the body but cannot kill the soul; rather fear him who can destroy both soul and body in hell. Are not two sparrows sold for a penny? Yet not one of them will fall to the ground unperceived by your Father. And even the hairs of your head are all counted. So do not be afraid; you are of more value than many sparrows.

'Everyone therefore who acknowledges me before others, I also will acknowledge before my Father in heaven; but whoever denies me before others, I also will deny before my Father in heaven.'

On Boxing Day I mentioned St Thomas Becket and the sermon that T. S. Eliot puts into his mouth as an interlude in the action of his play *Murder in the Cathedral*. But today we come back to Becket himself because it is today that we celebrate his feast day. Whereas the other feasts in the days immediately after Christmas Day are in some way related to the birth of Jesus – the first martyr, the theologian of the incarnation, the Holy Innocents – Becket's day is not like that. Instead it was on this day in 1170 that the Archbishop was murdered, martyred, in his cathedral in Canterbury by four knights who had ridden from London to do the king's business. They took his infamous words 'Who will rid me of this turbulent priest?' not as perhaps a rhetorical question but as a request, a command, thrown out into the air. You have to listen carefully and not take everything at face value; you have to speak carefully and consider the effect your words may have!

But whether or not Henry II really wanted Becket killed, the result was that one of the greatest saints in English history was created and, as a consequence, the greatest English shrine and focus for pilgrimage established.

I suppose Becket saw the ending as inevitable. He couldn't escape his assassins, the writing was on the wall, the script was written and as the swords descended on him I hope that fear left him.

The gospel reading for the Eucharist today has these powerful words:

Do not be afraid; you are of more value than many sparrows. (Matthew 10.31)

Fear is overwhelming. It can easily dominate our lives and stop us from acting. Fear can hold us back in life and mean that we cannot be the person that God desires us to be. I was a very fearful young man, shy, worried; it hampered my growing up, it stopped me enjoying life. There came a point of decision making for me – was I going to allow my life to be traumatized by fear, or was I going to let God be my courage? I had to choose God over my fears.

Travel forward in the Jesus story until after his resurrection. St John tells us that the disciples were in the Upper Room 'and the doors of the house ... were locked for fear of the Jews' (John 20.19). The Upper Room had become a prison for them; their fears were becoming a prison of their own making. But Jesus steps into that locked space of fear and breathes his peace upon them. Yet, even so, by Pentecost they are still in that room. And so the Holy Spirit comes and bursts open the windows and drives them into the streets and casts aside their fears so that they can speak.

St John in his First Letter writes:

There is no fear in love, but perfect love casts out fear. (1 John 4.18)

We have been Bethlehem bound, we travelled a long way for the birth of a child. But this is no ordinary child – this child is love and this love will cast out our fear. The poet Christina Rossetti wrote a poem which helps us with this:

Love came down at Christmas,
Love all lovely, Love Divine,
Love was born at Christmas,
Star and Angels gave the sign.

Worship we the Godhead,
Love Incarnate, Love Divine,
Worship we our Jesus,
But wherewith for sacred sign?

Love shall be our token,
Love be yours and love be mine,
Love to God and all men,
Love for plea and gift and sign.[16]

Love came down in Bethlehem and that love, perfect, casts out our fear. Challenge your fear with the love of God in Jesus and live the full life the child comes to bring.

Love divine,
Love, all perfect,
cast out my fear;
enter in
that I may live in you.
Amen.

And now meet ... Thomas

I was a boy, standing on Cheapside in the heart of bustling London, the church of St Mary-le-Bow in front of us, my father, Gilbert, on one side of me, my mother, Matilda, on the other. The king was due to pass by, making his way from the Tower of London, just outside the city walls, and then, with the blessing of the mayor and aldermen, through the City and past St Paul's to his palace in Westminster. The crowds lined the streets as they always did when the king was passing from one palace to another. The banners of the guilds were flapping in the breeze, the masters and their apprentices stood with pride in their livery, the street had been cleaned of the mess you found in Poultry. My heart missed a beat as the king passed and our eyes met, just for a moment.

I was a young man, in the Archbishop's palace across the river in Lambeth. I had been called to serve Archbishop Theobald, which was a joy. He trusted me and sent me as his envoy. But today he sent me on a special mission, back across the river: not to the City where I grew up, but to Westminster and to the palace we looked at from Lambeth. I was to be chancellor to the king. The throne room in which I waited was glorious, the carving, the tapestries, the courtiers, the banners all adding to the feeling of regal splendour. And, as the king entered with pages and attendants, his glory filling that chamber and the trumpets sounding, our eyes met, just for a moment. My heart missed a beat as I realized what a task was to be mine.

I am an older man, a priest, a bishop, an archbishop. I have been in exile, but have now been brought back. I was in favour then out of it. I have faced the king in his palace on the north bank from my palace on the south. But now was the time to leave. I preached a sermon to the Augustinians gathered in their Priory of St Mary Overie in Southwark and then, after enjoying their hospitality, made my final journey to Canterbury. I had watched one king, I had served one king; now I was serving another king, Jesus Christ, the king born in a manger, reigning from a cross, glorified in the heavenly courts. As it says in the Song of Songs, 'his banner over me was love'. I was praying with my brethren in the monastery, keeping the great Octave of Christmas, when the doors of the cathedral flew open and we heard the clink of armour and the sound of soldiers and I saw the candles reflected in the sharp steel of swords. I caught the eye of my heavenly king, just for a moment, and my heart missed a beat.

> Lord God,
> who gave grace to your servant Thomas Becket
> to put aside all earthly fear
> and be faithful even to death:
> grant that we, disregarding worldly esteem,
> may fight all wrong,
> uphold your rule,
> and serve you to our life's end;
> through Jesus Christ our Lord.
> Amen.[17]

30 December

Luke 2.36–40

> *There was also a prophet, Anna the daughter of Phanuel, of the tribe of Asher. She was of a great age, having lived with her husband for seven years after her marriage, then as a widow to the age of eighty-four. She never left the temple but worshipped there with fasting and prayer night and day. At that moment she came, and began to praise God and to speak about the child to all who were looking for the redemption of Jerusalem.*
>
> *When they had finished everything required by the law of the Lord, they returned to Galilee, to their own town of Nazareth. The child grew and became strong, filled with wisdom; and the favour of God was upon him.*

The story has moved on. This passage is from the end of the account of the presentation of Christ in the temple.

There are two principal characters in that story, apart from the Holy Family, Jesus, Mary and Joseph. Simeon was an old man, righteous and devout, who looked for the coming of the one God had promised. Then there was Anna, a prophet, who features in this passage.

I love Anna. I love the way we are given a little story of her life. Even by the standards of our own society in which we can all expect to live so much longer, Anna was doing very well. Sixty may be the new 40 but 84 is still not bad going. And we can imagine that, having only been married for seven years before being widowed, life will have been hard. She may well have been supported, as a widow, by family and friends – but maybe not.

When the early church was being formed there was the need to create an order of ministers to do the pastoral, servant ministry of the church. Stephen, whose feast day we celebrated on Boxing Day, was one of that first group of deacons. Their task was to look after the poor, and we are told that there was a particular issue that faced the community with regard to widows and the daily distribution of food (Acts 6.1). St Paul, writing later to the infant churches, often turns his attention to widows, how they should behave, who should look after them. Widows were high on the agenda of the church because they could be a completely unsupported group in society.

So Anna may have had it hard. But she was obviously a survivor. She spent all her time in the temple and she was a prophet; she fasted and prayed all the time. So we can imagine that people knew her and people listened to her. In the account of the Presentation, Anna comes on to the scene and praises God and speaks. But then she does something else.

I used to go to Launde Abbey in Leicestershire as a teenager for my retreats. I distinctly remember one of those retreats and what was said, though, sadly, I can't remember the name of the priest who was leading us. But he told us – and I liked this so much that I had to write it on a piece of paper and put it up on the noticeboard in my room at home – that we were to 'keep the rumour of God alive'.

Rumours spread, very quickly – ever more quickly, thanks to social media. You can fuel a rumour, keep it going, keep it alive. The retreat conductor used that word 'rumour' in a way that caught our attention, certainly caught my attention – 'Keep the rumour of God alive.'

This is what Anna does. She goes off and tells those who would listen, those who like her and Simeon were looking for the redemption of Jerusalem, that the redeemer had come, that God's promise had been fulfilled, that a child had been born. She kept the rumour alive.

We might call it mission, we might call it evangelism, we might simply call it telling other people about Jesus. The church needs to be a rumour-mill for Christ, keeping the story going, keeping the truth being told, learning from a woman of experience and spreading the word. We made the journey to Bethlehem to see a child. Don't keep it to yourself – tell others what you know of God. Keep the rumour of God alive.

> Lord, as you gave Anna the passion to speak of you,
> give us that same desire
> to tell others of you
> and your love,
> to keep the rumour alive.
> Amen.

And now meet ... Anna

You have all been Bethlehem bound. I can't remember, to be honest, the last time I was in Bethlehem. Maybe it was in those few years of my marriage. I was a young girl then and my husband had relatives around the Jerusalem area, so we probably went there then. He was a priest, so we needed to be in the area of the temple for those times when he was on duty. Some of the priests lived down in Jericho: they made their way from that lovely warm place into the city when they needed to be there and at other times spent their time among the date palms, reading, writing, translating. But we decided to stay in the place we were familiar with. It was a good thing really, as after just seven years he was dead and I was a widow – without children.

In many ways it has been a hard life; people aren't as kind as they might be to childless widows. But I have never been one to want too much – a good thing really because I have never had much. In fact the temple is everything I need.

I was taken there by my father Phanuel. He was a prophet, and as his only child I would follow him into the courts and hang on his cloak and his every word. He was such a powerful speaker; I just loved listening to him.

I loved his name, Phanuel. It might seem strange to you, but everyone who heard it knew that it meant 'the face of God': the name of one of the archangels, the name of the place where our ancestor Jacob met with God, wrestled with him overnight and saw his face. Face to face with God. I am my father's daughter. People call me a prophet, and that is good because they help me survive. It is meant to be a blessing to help a prophet, with a cup of water, with a piece of bread. I don't look for much and for what I am given I am truly thankful.

But I do look for the face of God. I long to see God face to face, to live up to my father's name, to do as my husband did, as far as I can as a woman, to speak of God to those who will listen. That's why I never leave the temple. This is God's house and, basically, I live here. It never really closes, and everyone is used to seeing me now. That's why I travel nowhere – because I don't want to miss the sight of God.

Another prophet, Malachi, said this: 'The LORD, whom you seek, shall suddenly come to his temple.' It will be sudden, so I can't be anywhere else. I look for the face of God, and wait, because I am Phanuel's daughter.

> Loving God,
> may I watch for you
> in all around me,
> and see your face
> in my sister,
> in my brother,
> in the sudden stranger.
> Amen.

31 December

John 1.1–18

In the beginning was the Word, and the Word was with God, and the Word was God. He was in the beginning with God. All things came into being through him, and without him not one thing came into being. What has come into being in him was life, and the life was the light of all people. The light shines in the darkness, and the darkness did not overcome it.

There was a man sent from God, whose name was John. He came as a witness to testify to the light, so that all might believe through him. He himself was not the light, but he came to testify to the light. The true light, which enlightens everyone, was coming into the world.

He was in the world, and the world came into being through him; yet the world did not know him. He came to what was his own, and his own people did not accept him. But to all who received him, who believed in his name, he gave power to become children of God, who were born, not of blood or of the will of the flesh or of the will of man, but of God.

And the Word became flesh and lived among us, and we have seen his glory, the glory as of a father's only son, full of grace and truth. (John testified to him and cried out, 'This was he of whom I said, "He who comes after me ranks ahead of me because he was before me."') From his fullness we have all received, grace upon grace. The law indeed was given through Moses; grace and truth came through Jesus Christ. No one has ever seen God. It is God the only Son, who is close to the Father's heart, who has made him known.

It's almost a week since we first heard this gospel read at the Christmas Day Eucharist but we return to it today. In fact, this is a longer passage from the beginning of St John's Gospel than we get on Christmas Day. We are given those extra verses.

The five senses are such an important part of who we are as human beings and how we relate to the world. While I was at primary school in Leicester we read the story of Helen Keller. I remember it having a profound effect upon me. I think, at that stage, I hadn't really encountered anyone who had extreme forms of sight or hearing impairment, no one deaf or blind. We heard about them in church, of course, because so many of the miracles recorded in the Gospels seem to be about giving people back their senses. But at that time in my life it wasn't my own experience. And so to read of this young girl who was deafblind and as a consequence initially had no language skills at all was amazingly moving. Her teacher, Anne Sullivan, liberated her, teaching her language skills so that eventually Helen was the first deafblind person to be awarded a Bachelor of Arts degree.

I remember reading how Anne taught Helen that each object has a name that we learn. She poured water over her hands while spelling the word 'water' on her palm. All of a sudden the penny dropped. Anne broke through into Helen's isolation and she became able to learn and to communicate. Of course, for her the sense of touch was a way of breaking through where other senses were denying her access to the world. We can only wonder at those individuals who suffer complete sensory deprivation in which nothing from beyond them can have any effect. It is the kind of thing that people inflict on others as a form of torture – but some of our brothers and sisters are living this life day in, day out.

When on our journey we arrived at Bethlehem we saw a baby in a manger. That was the object of our journey, to see this Holy Child. That is the wonder of the incarnation, of course, that in Jesus we can experience with our senses the God who is beyond the spheres of taste, sound, touch, sight and smell with which we know and experience the world.

St John describes this in the gospel reading for today:

> No one has ever seen God. It is God the only Son, who is close to the Father's heart, who has made him known. (John 1.18)

The God whom we had been unable to see, we see in Jesus; the God whom we had been unable to touch, we touch in Jesus. And the same can be said for each of the five senses with which we have been blessed. In Jesus our experience, our direct experience of the Godhead, of divinity, becomes complete. As Helen felt the water running through her fingers and learned the name by which it is called, so we touch God and learn God's name, God's reality.

In his First Letter St John writes:

> *We declare to you what was from the beginning, what we have heard, what we have seen with our eyes, what we have looked at and touched with our hands.* (1 John 1.1)

John speaks of a total experience of God through the incarnation. But you may say that that was then and this is now. We have been to Bethlehem in heart and mind, in prayer, Bethlehem bound as a community, but we couldn't touch and see and hear as John is saying. But that is where the sacramental life of the church is so important. The incarnation and the sacraments are part of the same encounter with God.

As God in Jesus took flesh, so the whole of the sentient world was touched with the divine. God could be experienced in another way, a more intimate, direct way than before. And that of course is the life of the church. Through outward visible signs we experience inward spiritual grace in each of the sacraments. In the dominical sacraments, those given to us directly by the Lord, baptism and the Eucharist, in water and in bread and wine, our senses are brought into contact with God and the reality of God becomes part of the reality of our lives. Through the other five sacraments of the church (one of the extravagant riches of God which John in this gospel reading calls 'grace upon grace' is that there are more sacraments than senses) we experience the touch and sign of the divine for every part of our lives.

There is a sense in which humanity before the incarnation was as locked away as was Helen Keller, but as her teacher broke through and liberated her from her prison of isolation, so in Jesus we have been liberated and brought into a new and sensitive relationship with God. As I hold the bread in my hands there is a real sense that I am holding Christ, as though my Bethlehem journey had enabled me to truly pick the child from the manger and love him as I would want to do.

God confronts me as I look into the crib and God confronts my sight, my sound, my taste, my touch, what I smell; God is all around me as well as within me. This is part of the glory of Christmas that is renewed every time I approach God in the sacramental life of the church and in more ways as well. For as Evelyn Underhill wrote:

> *God is always coming to you in the Sacrament of the Present Moment. Meet and receive Him there with gratitude in that sacrament.*[18]

I would add, with gratitude in every sacrament, for each is an encounter with the God we know in Jesus who enters every present moment through the mystery of the incarnation.

Lord God,
through sight and sound,
through touch and taste,
through my sense of smell,
may I experience you
and know you
and love you.
Amen.

And now meet ...
the Innkeeper's Wife

It has been a long but beautiful week. I have to admit I'm exhausted – and it's not that I shy away from hard work, but there has been a huge amount to do. But, even though I could just drop to sleep at a moment's notice, I'm so happy.

You met my husband; I leave front-of-house to him. I'm the behind-the-scenes person. He likes playing the host, the 'nothing is too much trouble' welcoming face of our little inn. Well, as I say to him, it might not be too much trouble for you but it's me who has to do the work. That's the trouble with men, they like the limelight but leave the hard work to us women.

But I have to admit now that he did the right thing, when there was that knock on the door and he opened it to find Joseph standing there, exhausted, stressed out, with his young wife Mary on the donkey. I was listening to what my husband said, disapproving to be honest, and concerned. Clearly she was about to give birth and a stable wasn't a fit place for that to happen. But the offer was made and, desperate, they accepted it. Then later on another knock: the baby was coming, could I help.

I have had a few of my own and looked over the shoulders of the midwives at other confinements so I knew what to do. And the baby came quickly and easily. I had brought some cloth with me and I bound the baby tightly in the swaddling and gave him back to his mother. There was silence, no words, just an intense feeling of love, not just Mary's love for her son – it was a little boy – but an all-encompassing love that seemed to touch every one of my senses, almost overwhelming. I'd never experienced love like it.

The rest of the evening was odd to say the least. Some of those shepherds came down, off the hills, with wild stories of angels. But even though they're not my kind of people it seemed that they were also overwhelmed by love. When they left as the first streaks of dawn lit up the sky it wasn't like the drunken rabble they usually are; they weren't waking up the neighbourhood with their coarse words and singing, but instead with good news of this baby.

The inn is empty now. As soon as the count had happened everyone went back to their hometowns, to the places they'd come from. My husband is counting the takings, he seems very happy. I have cooked everything we have and need to go to market. But the family are still in the stable. And that feeling of love is still there.

I spend a lot of time with Mary, in between my chores, talking. I take my time with the baby, as she gets some sleep. I hold him close, like one of my own, while Joseph helps my husband with those little repair jobs that he has never got round to doing! Men!

I can't bear for them to leave. Holding this baby is like ... holding all life in my hands.

> Lord Jesus,
> love come down,
> hold my life
> as I hold yours.
> Amen.

1 January

Luke 2.15–21

When the angels had left them and gone into heaven, the shepherds said to one another, 'Let us go now to Bethlehem and see this thing that has taken place, which the Lord has made known to us.' So they went with haste and found Mary and Joseph, and the child lying in the manger. When they saw this, they made known what had been told them about this child; and all who heard it were amazed at what the shepherds told them. But Mary treasured all these words and pondered them in her heart. The shepherds returned, glorifying and prais-

ing God for all they had heard and seen, as it had been told them.

After eight days had passed, it was time to circumcise the child; and he was called Jesus, the name given by the angel before he was conceived in the womb.

New Year's Day has, potentially, three titles in the church calendar. Two come from the gospel for the day and the third is a more general celebration. In the Anglican calendar we can call today 'The Feast of the Circumcision of Christ' or 'The Feast of the Naming of Jesus'. In the Roman Catholic calendar, however, it is called 'The Feast of Mary the Mother of God'. That last title refers back to the declaration at the Council of Ephesus in 431 AD of Mary as 'Theotokos', a word that means 'God-bearer' – hence the title 'Mother of God'. For some more sensitive Christian souls this sounds an over-the-top title. How can God have a mother? The pre-existent God surely cannot come from human origin, 'born of a woman, born under the law' as Paul describes it (Galatians 4.4)? But this title for Mary draws us into that deeper truth that the child whom we have visited in the manger in Bethlehem, the focus and destination of our journey when we were Bethlehem bound, is a baby who not only will become the greatest man, but is the incarnate Son of God, God sharing our humanity.

Jesus in his divine nature is God; Mary bore him in her womb; therefore she is Theotokos, the God-bearer, and we can, consequently and rightly, name her as Mother of God.

But it wasn't this that I particularly wanted to think about today. The other names we can give to this day are more important in that they have a scriptural resonance associated with this day itself, as opposed to celebrating something which is purely doctrinal in nature.

One year in the middle of Advent, one of the young couples in the congregation at Southwark Cathedral gave birth to a baby. I had actually married them earlier in the year and we were all delighted when we heard that they were expecting a baby. So the baby was safely born; and I then received the message that they would want the 'Eighth Day' naming ceremony. The husband is of Nigerian heritage, and in accordance with the tradition back in Nigeria, and in many other countries, it was important that the new parents, with the rest of the family, came along to church on the Eighth Day to name the child and give thanks for his birth and safe delivery. I had officiated at the ceremony on other occasions and so was delighted but not surprised.

So we gathered in the Harvard Chapel on the morning of the eighth day – miraculously we found an hour when there wasn't a carol service going on – and I read this gospel before we named the child. Sebastian Tomilayo was the name chosen by the parents and we gave thanks for his life. There was, of course, an English tradition of giving thanks after the birth of a child which was called 'The Churching of Women' in the Book of Common Prayer. But for various reasons, especially an erroneous idea that childbirth made a woman unclean and in need of cleansing before she could be reintegrated into society, it fell out of use. That also meant that this healthy and wonderful ceremony – which linked us back to this event in the life of Jesus and back further into Old Testament traditions – of giving thanks for a safe delivery and naming the new child, has become uncommon in contemporary society.

But as we stood in the chapel with little Sebastian Tomilayo in our arms we were able to remember that a safe birth is a little miracle and needs to be acknowledged as such; and for the whole family gathered before God it was the acknowledgement of a new beginning, a new family and the blessing that that brings.

As with the story of the naming of John that we thought about before Christmas, the name that Joseph and Mary gave to their child was preordained. Gabriel had told Mary, just as Zechariah had been told, what she was to call the child. 'You will name him Jesus,' said Gabriel. We're not told that when the naming ceremony came along there was the kind of questioning that happened on the eighth day with John. But presumably that was because Mary and Joseph were away from their home environment, from Nazareth where they were known, in this place in which they were relative strangers, and so no one could say 'But no one in your family has this name.'

Sebastian Tomilayo's parents had chosen the name carefully – Tomilayo is a Yoruba name that is translated 'My joy' – and the name that the angel gave to Mary was important. The name Jesus shares the same roots as the name Joshua. It was Joshua who did what Moses could not do – he took the children of Israel across the Jordan into the Promised Land. The name, Jesus, Joshua, Jeshua in Hebrew means 'God saves'. As the angel said to Joseph at the beginning of St Matthew's Gospel of the child to be born to Mary, 'he will save his people from their sins'. It was all in the name.

For us that holy name is everything. After his death and resurrection, after the day of Pentecost, the apostles are witnessing to Christ in the world and they are healing the sick. Peter is arrested for doing just that and is asked about his authority for acting in this way. Peter responds with characteristic boldness:

'There is salvation in no one else, for there is no other name under heaven given among mortals by which we must be saved.' (Acts 4.12)

This name, given on this day, is the name at which heads must bow, the name written on our hearts. This is the name by which we will be saved, the name above all other names. This is Jesus, Saviour, who will take us across another Jordan to the land of God's promise.

Lord Jesus Christ, Son of God,
have mercy on me, a sinner.
Amen.[19]

And now meet ... the Elder

Some of them call me Rabbi, some of them call me 'the Elder', all I know is that I was elected by the other men to lead our synagogue in Bethlehem. We were close to Jerusalem and the temple but we also liked to gather to pray and, as there were more than ten of us, we were allowed to set up this *minyan*, this gathering. We knew each other well, we had all grown up here. But it is lovely, nevertheless, when someone else joins us.

Bethlehem was settling back down after a few days of frantic busyness. Many people had been Bethlehem bound, responding to the instruction from the Romans that every man had to be in his ancestral home to be registered and counted. And, as the hometown of King David, there were many who needed to come back here.

Now things are pretty much back to normal. At my age there's little for me to do. I sit in the square and talk to the men I grew up with, while my sons do the work, looking after the barley harvest and getting the grain to the millers and the bakers. This after all is a town named after its principal trade: this is the 'House of Bread' and our barley is some of the finest in the region – or at least I like to think it is.

Of course, I also go into the synagogue seven times a day to lead the prayers. As our ancestor David wrote in the Psalms, 'Seven times a day do I praise thee because of thy righteous judgments.' Then today, just after our midday prayers some strangers came in. It was a man and a young girl and she was carrying a baby. I hadn't seen them before but as soon as he spoke I could tell they weren't from these parts.

He said that their baby was eight days old. It was the day to give the baby his name and to circumcise him so that he was fully part of our people, the children of Abraham, who circumcised his own son in obedience to the command of God.

'What is his name?' I asked.

'Jesus,' he said.

'Jesus,' she said.

'Jesus he shall be,' I responded. A lovely name, strong, hopeful, courageous like our ancestor who brought our people across the water, from slavery to freedom in this Promised Land.

I took the knife from where we kept it, for this very task. The mother looked away, they always do in my experience, not wanting to see their baby shed blood, not wanting to hear the cry. But the father looked on, proud of his son, proud of our heritage, proud to be a Jew. The blood was shed, the baby cried, it was over in an instant. The mother with tenderness wiped the blood away, hoping in her heart that he wouldn't have to shed more blood in his life, and bound the baby back into his swaddling.

Then they left. I saw him – Joseph – again, he would join us for prayers. He was a carpenter by trade, we discovered,

and I was right: he was from the north, and a good man.
She kept herself to herself, with the baby, her treasure.

> Almighty God,
> whose blessed Son was circumcised
> in obedience to the law for our sake
> and given the Name that is above every name:
> give us grace faithfully to bear his Name,
> to worship him in the freedom of the Spirit,
> and to proclaim him as the Saviour of the world;
> who is alive and reigns with you,
> in the unity of the Holy Spirit,
> one God, now and for ever.
> Amen.[20]

2 January

John 1.19–28

This is the testimony given by John when the Jews sent priests and Levites from Jerusalem to ask him, 'Who are you?' He confessed and did not deny it, but confessed, 'I am not the Messiah.' And they asked him, 'What then? Are you Elijah?' He said, 'I am not.' 'Are you the prophet?' He answered, 'No.' Then they said to him, 'Who are you? Let us have an answer for those who sent us. What do you say about yourself?' He said,

'*I am the voice of one crying out in the wilderness,*

"Make straight the way of the Lord"',

as the prophet Isaiah said.

Now they had been sent from the Pharisees. They asked him, 'Why then are you baptizing if you are neither the Messiah, nor Elijah, nor the prophet?' John answered them, 'I baptize with water. Among you stands one whom you do not know, the one who is coming after me; I am not worthy to untie the thong of his sandal.' This took place in Bethany across the Jordan where John was baptizing.

Yesterday was an important stage in the Christmas story. The eighth day is of course the Octave Day and part of the Christian tradition – though it may go back in origin to the eight-day Feast of Tabernacles in the Jewish tradition. Similarly, the celebration of Easter extends until and includes the Sunday after Easter, and each of the days is celebrated with equal solemnity. But Christmas goes even beyond the eight days.

The traditional and much-loved Christmas carol, 'The Twelve Days of Christmas' refers to this. The initial celebration of Christmas extends for a full 12 days because it concludes with the Feast of the Epiphany – the Manifestation of Christ to the Gentiles – on 6 January. That is still to come and it will bring the feasting and the revelling, along with our journey to Bethlehem, to its conclusion.

For the journey is not yet over. There are people still Bethlehem bound, a group of them travelling from the east on their way to see this thing that has happened. They have been summoned, not by angels but by a star, and in response they have left their foreign homeland and made the long and treacherous journey to – they know not where. But, while at this stage we acknowledge that they are on their way, we leave them for a while.

Instead the gospel for the Eucharist today takes us beyond Bethlehem, shepherds, wise men and angels and to the very beginning of Jesus' public ministry. John takes us to the banks of the Jordan. Yesterday I was reflecting on the name that the baby in the manger was given, the name 'Jesus'. It is a name that resonates with that great figure of Jewish history, Joshua, who saw the children of Israel across the River Jordan and into the land that God had promised them when they were slaves in Egypt. Crossing the Jordan was their entry into freedom and the end of their wanderings – for this stage in their history at least.

John the Evangelist takes us to the banks of the Jordan, and we meet someone else who has already featured heavily in this journey to Bethlehem. John the Baptist has left his home and his parents, Elizabeth and Zechariah. He is now in the desert, somewhere in the Judean wilderness.

There are many 'traditional' baptismal sites on the modern-day Jordan. One thing that always strikes me though when I go to the Jordan, to any of the sites, during a pilgrimage, to celebrate the 'Reaffirmation of Baptismal Promises' is, frankly, how unimpressive the Jordan is.

I've been very fortunate to live alongside the River Thames. Now that is a river! The modern Jordan is a rather pathetic stream of brown and unappealing water. It is quite unattractive to be honest, yet pilgrims go down to its muddy edge to remember their own baptism and to grab a little of the water to take home with them. The truth is that too much of the water is grabbed – not by eager pilgrims but by the farmers on the Jordan valley. The valley is now green and productive, producing cash crops for the Israeli home and international markets, and it is the Jordan that is providing the water for irrigation.

When John was there, and the crowds were gathering round him to hear his uncompromising preaching and to receive baptism for repentance at his hands, we would imagine that the Jordan was much more of a river than a stream (although Naaman's reluctance to bathe in it to cure him of his leprosy in 2 Kings 5 might suggest it was always less than impressive). The gospel takes us into a situation in which people are trying to find out just who John is. Just as later, at Caesarea Philippi, Jesus will ask his disciples who people say that he is, the people quizzing John come out with the same suggestions – the Messiah, Elijah, the prophet? To each John answers 'No'.

But then he says something wonderful:

> *'Among you stands one whom you do not know.'*
> (John 1.26)

There, somewhere in the crowds, is Jesus, but as yet no one knows him. Perhaps John hasn't seen him yet himself. Perhaps the last time they met was when their mothers greeted each other, and the unborn John leapt in recognition. John now looks into the crowd with eager anticipation, waiting for his heart to leap again. 'Among you stands one whom you do not know.'

The journey to Bethlehem has been the journey to look into the crib and see Jesus. But Jesus is no longer in the crib, he is alongside us and we often don't recognize him. Even though we are devoted to him, even though we have made this journey, yet we can still sometimes miss him in the crowd.

In St Matthew's Gospel even the righteous say to the Lord:

> Lord, *when was it that we saw you hungry and gave you food, or thirsty and gave you something to drink? And when was it that we saw you a stranger and welcomed you, or naked and gave you clothing? And when was it that we saw you sick or in prison and visited you?* (Matthew 25.37–39)

Just as children will spend hours looking into the complicated pictures in a *Where's Wally?* book and not find him, so we can so often miss Jesus in the crowd. Yet he is there, alongside us, with us, God with us; known yet so often unknown, seen yet so often unseen, recognized yet so often unrecognized.

Lord Jesus,
open my eyes
that I may see you,
serve you,
love you,
today.
Amen.

And now meet ... John

We haven't actually met before, well not properly. You have heard about me, many times already, but we haven't actually met. My name is John. Oddly, it was a name not chosen by my parents but given at the command of God, through an angel. Incredible. My parents, Zechariah and Elizabeth, told me the story, how my father didn't believe the angel, how he was struck dumb, how I was born and what happened on the eighth day as he wrote 'His name is John' and the scandal that caused in the neighbourhood. He got his voice back, though, and would often sing about it. So that's who I am, though oddly people just seem to call me 'the Baptist', not John!

My parents were quite old when I was born – another odd thing – so apart from the stories about how I got my name, and a visit my mother had from her cousin Mary that they would tell me about, I don't remember much about them. They died while I was still young, and not having many relatives in the area I was taken down into the desert and placed in the care of a group of men who lived out their life there in a community. I was to learn that they were called the Essenes.

It was a hard life but a good one. My brothers didn't go in for comforts – no rich robes, no palaces – but we had the most fantastic library and all the writings, on scrolls, were stored in clay jars with the most wonderful lids in the dry caves around where we lived. I would go and sit with one of the elder brethren and read with him, from the prophets, about our life, about the struggles between light and dark and all that would come in the future.

But one thing frustrated me. We were isolated, and if we knew all this stuff shouldn't we tell other people, warn other people, get other people to change their lives, to wash off their sins as we did every day in our *mikveh*, one of our ritual pools? I'd argue this out with the others, but they wanted to stay where they were, as they were. So, in the end, I left and made my way north, along the banks of the Dead Sea and to the River Jordan.

Word spreads quickly. People make their way all the time along the wilderness road between Jericho, close to where I lived, and Jerusalem in the hills. From just a few listening to me at first, being willing to step into the flowing water, the living water, with me and be washed, crowds began to gather. Those crowds brought so many different kinds of people – soldiers, lawyers, tax collectors and ordinary folk. But I didn't care who they were, I told them straight – not all of them liked it, but I told them – 'Change your ways', and the water was full of people washing.

My mother's cousin had a son, just a little younger than me. I've never met him, don't know how I'd recognize him, but I wonder if he will come when he hears what his wild, untamed relative is doing. But, you know, I have a feeling I will know him when I see him.

> Loving God,
> forgive me my sins
> and make me holy to serve you in the world,
> through Jesus Christ our Lord.
> Amen.[21]

3 January

John 1.29–34

The next day he saw Jesus coming towards him and declared, 'Here is the Lamb of God who takes away the sin of the world! This is he of whom I said, "After me comes a man who ranks ahead of me because he was before me." I myself did not know him; but I came baptizing with water for this reason, that he might be revealed to Israel.' And John testified, 'I saw the Spirit descending from heaven like a dove, and it remained on him. I myself did not know him, but the one who sent me to baptize with water said to me, "He on whom you see the Spirit descend and remain is the one who baptizes with the Holy Spirit." And I myself have seen and have testified that this is the Son of God.'

And then he saw him, coming through the crowds. He had been watching the people, expecting Jesus to be among them, and all of a sudden there he was. As in that first prenatal meeting his heart must have leapt in recognition. The forerunner, the preparer of the way, John, the wild prophet in the wilderness, saw the one for whom he had been preparing the people.

But instead of some great cry of greeting, instead of some declaration of 'Here he is – I told you he was coming', the Evangelist gives us other words from the Baptist:

> *'Here is the Lamb of God who takes away the sin of the world!'* (John 1.29)

Those words in Latin, *'Ecce Agnus Dei'*, 'This is the Lamb of God', are the words traditionally used as we are invited to move to the altar and receive Holy Communion. The priest holds the host before the people as the words are said, so that our attention is drawn in a powerful way to the bread held up for us to see, the bread that is the Body of Christ.

I was taught to pray by my mother. Each day, before we went to sleep, ended with some prayers, mostly intercessory and, of course, commending ourselves to the love of God. Mum insisted that we put our hands together and closed our eyes. According to her that was the way to pray, that was the position one should adopt for prayer. And that was reinforced in Sunday school and at day school. 'Put your hands together and close your eyes ... Let us pray', said the headmistress. There we all were in the assembly hall, sitting cross-legged, eyes closed, hands together.

It was good training of course, because what Mum and the rest of those teaching me were saying was, don't get distracted while you're praying. 'Hands together' stops little ones fidgeting; 'eyes closed' stops little ones looking. But go to the catacombs in Rome and you will see early Christian frescos showing another way of praying, standing up, arms stretched out, hands lifted up. It looks much more alert than the ranks of the obedient unseeing kids in our school!

And this moment of presentation, of call, of recognition in the Eucharist is definitely not one when you should have your eyes closed. This is an 'eyes wide open' moment in the liturgy. The priest shows us the host and there is a command to look, to recognize and to respond. Whatever the words are in the liturgy we are familiar with – 'This is ...', 'Behold ...', even the Anglican 'Jesus is ...' (which, conveniently for some Anglicans, sidesteps the thorny issue of whether the priest is talking about the host or about Jesus in general!) – we are called to look and to recognize. And that was what John the Baptist was doing, there in the wilderness, by the Jordan, as Jesus stepped out from the crowd and into public recognition and public ministry.

At the Royal Variety Performance at the London Palladium, the compere announcing the main act steps back into the wings. This moment is the beginning of John stepping back, his job almost done. A couple of chapters later, John the Baptist, speaking to his own disciples about Jesus, says:

'He must increase, but I must decrease.' (John 3.30)

John steps to one side and the Lamb moves into the centre of the stage.

That image, of course, of Jesus as the Lamb of God is one of the most powerful and enduring. It speaks to us of the sacrifice that will be offered by the one for whom we have been Bethlehem bound, the one for whom shepherds left their flocks. William Blake wrote that most beautiful poem, hauntingly set to music by Sir John Tavener, in his collection *Songs of Innocence and Experience*. The collection is made up of mirror images of poems in the two sections. 'The Lamb' mirrors that other great poem 'The Tyger'. But his poem 'The Lamb' reflects so beautifully the intimate relationship that we have with the Lamb of God to whom John points.

Little Lamb, who made thee?
Dost thou know who made thee?
Gave thee life, and bid thee feed,
By the stream and o'er the mead;
Gave thee clothing of delight,
Softest clothing, woolly, bright;
Gave thee such a tender voice,
Making all the vales rejoice?
Little Lamb, who made thee?
Dost thou know who made thee?

Little Lamb, I'll tell thee,
Little Lamb, I'll tell thee.
He is called by thy name,
For He calls Himself a Lamb.
He is meek, and He is mild;
He became a little child.
I a child, and thou a lamb,
We are called by His name.
Little Lamb, God bless thee!
Little Lamb, God bless thee![22]

There is a time to close one's eyes and pray, but there are times to look and see and pray and not miss the Lamb in the crowds.

> Lamb of God, you take away the sin of the world,
>   have mercy on us.
> Lamb of God, you take away the sin of the world,
>   have mercy on us.
> Lamb of God, you take away the sin of the world,
>   grant us peace.
> Amen.

And now meet ... Melchior

I was standing in the temple. My hands were lifted in prayer. The fire was alight and the shadows its burning created fell across the space. I had lived my life in the worship of Zoroaster and in the practice of good thoughts and good words to ensure happiness, not just for me but for the whole of creation and to keep chaos at bay. When I stepped out of the fire-lit temple it was dark, an inky deep darkness. You could call me a night-owl really. I catch up with sleep during the day, but I spend my night times outside, looking at the black sky above, looking at the stars, searching them, reading them.

I am an old man now and so I know these skies and these stars so well. I have watched them move in their patterns and orbits for so many years. I have marvelled as stars have shot across the firmament. I have seen the comets, appearing with regularity, and I have kept a note of when they come and where I will see them. I recognize the Zodiac, what God has written in the stars: a lion, twins, a crab, fish and the rest. I know the Plough, Orion's belt, they are like familiar friends to me.

And, because I have done this for so long, watched the stars and read them, people come to me, and ask me to read them for them, and they leave me with gifts. I am not short of gold. So I sit, no longer on the sands of the desert but on the terrace of my house, with soft cushions and glasses of sherbet and the sound of the shoes of my servants on the marble floors, and the deep blue of the lapis lazuli decorating the walls, brought by traders from the mountains in the north. The blue is the colour of heaven, the gold is the colour of the stars.

From my place of comfort I watched. I am seldom surprised nowadays; I have seen it all before. But suddenly I looked and looked again, for there was something new. There was a star I had never seen before, in a place I had never seen before. It was moving: not with the speed of a shooting star, not with the arc of a comet, but with a dignity I had never witnessed.

I looked at my notes and the records that others had left, those who had taught me to read the stars. But nothing; nothing resembling this. I spent that whole night watching.

In a strange way I felt it was telling me something. I felt as though I needed to travel, to follow it, to learn more. So when dawn came, and against my better instincts – I now prefer my home comforts – the servants loaded the camels, packed the finest tents, the best tapestries, the softest cushions, selected wine and dates and my best robes, and we set off.

Where I am bound I do not know. But I have my gold with me, just in case.

> Lord, may I follow your path
> even when I am not sure where it will lead me.
> Amen.

4 January

John 1.10–18

He was in the world, and the world came into being through him; yet the world did not know him. He came to what was his own, and his own people did not accept him. But to all who received him, who believed in his name, he gave power to become children of God, who were born, not of blood or of the will of the flesh or of the will of man, but of God.

And the Word became flesh and lived among us, and we have seen his glory, the glory as of a father's only son, full of grace and truth. (John testified to him and cried out, 'This was he of whom I said, "He who comes after me ranks ahead of me because he was before me."') From his fullness we have all received, grace upon grace.

The law indeed was given through Moses; grace and truth came through Jesus Christ. No one has ever seen God. It is God the only Son, who is close to the Father's heart, who has made him known.

We are back to that Christmas gospel again, the passage that opens St John's Gospel and which acts as the climax to so many carol services. The story goes that when King George II heard the 'Hallelujah Chorus' from Handel's *Messiah* performed, he stood and consequently everyone else stood. It became a tradition; it's a piece of music that we all stand for. In a similar way, in many carol services when we arrive at this, so often the final reading, we stand – it is that important.

But you can't read or hear this particular reading too often. There is always something that leaps out at you, grabs your attention, and that is the glory of scripture which we revisit again and again and again. Like the householder in the parable bringing from the storehouse 'things old and things new' we continually draw fresh water from the spring of scripture. We need that spring, that 'living water' as Jesus will describe it later in St John's Gospel.

What struck me as I read this again were the lines with which this gospel reading opens.

He was in the world, and the world came into being through him; yet the world did not know him. He came to what was his own, and his own people did not accept him. (John 1.10–11)

There is a marvellous passage in the book of Proverbs which ends like this:

I was beside him, like a master worker;
and I was daily his delight,
    rejoicing before him always,
rejoicing in his inhabited world
    and delighting in the human race.
(Proverbs 8.30–31)

The passage is about Wisdom, but it is often used to refer to the eternal nature of the Son, the second person of the Trinity whose incarnation we celebrate at this time and of which John so eloquently speaks. 'The world came into being through him,' says John, and the writer of the book of Proverbs suggests something similar.

I am a devotee of the work of R. S. Thomas. I know his poems can be a bit on the gloomy side but there is something for me about the way in which his questioning approach to faith draws out great truth in which we can all share. His poem 'The Coming' speaks of similar things to what we are thinking about, articulating as it does the desire of the Son to be among humankind.

'He came to what was his own, and his own people did not accept him', writes St John. With Jesus we are never far from the cross. While the visitors with whom we have been Bethlehem bound – and there are some still on their way – have in the main been happy to see the baby in the crib, not all of them have been, as we have seen. Herod was so paranoid that the slaughter of the innocents happened as a consequence. At Jesus' presentation in the temple, a feast that properly brings Christmas to a close, Simeon will take the child in his arms and say to his mother Mary:

'This child is destined for the falling and the rising of many in Israel, and to be a sign that will be opposed so that the inner thoughts of many will be revealed – and a sword will pierce your own soul too.' (Luke 2.34–35)

The Pre-Raphaelite artist John Everett Millais painted what was at the time a controversial picture called *Christ in the House of his Parents*. He pictures Jesus at work alongside his father, but this time it is Joseph; he is not, as Proverbs describes him, at the side of the creator God – 'I was beside him, like a master worker'. This is not cosmic creation but the work of the carpenter. And there in the workshop we see the materials for the cross and the tools and the nails that will ultimately hold Jesus to the wood. He has wounded his hand and Mary is on her knees caring for him – 'and a sword will pierce your own soul too'. You can see the painting in Tate Britain, and it is well worth a visit if you are in London.

We are never far from the cross and that is what R. S. Thomas hints at in his poem – 'Let me go there'. We continue to celebrate the fact that the Father sent the Son to be with us, one with us, to save his people from their sins from the wood of the crib to the wood of the cross.

Lord Jesus,
in the crib and on the cross
you were held by wood
and given the name above every name.
May your name
be written on my heart;
may my name
be written in your love.
Amen.

And now meet ... Caspar

I may seem a bit young to be a 'wise man', not as grey-haired as you thought I might be. The general view seems to be that wisdom comes with age. But I don't think that's always true and in fact, while I'm not quite as old as some of the other Magi with whom I minister, I am old enough to be a Magus. To be honest, with me it's not so much age as experience.

As a young boy I was given into the care of the wise men. My parents wanted me to be well educated, well cared for, something that they couldn't provide. So I was brought to the temple and left there. The story may sound familiar, I suspect it has happened to other young children. There were simple jobs that needed doing and youngsters like me could get on with them while the other Magi went about their priestly tasks, engaged in their studies, or sat staring at the stars.

Some of the other boys looked after the Holy Fire that was at the centre of our lives. It was my job, however, to make sure that the bowls of incense were always full, so that incense could be offered whenever the priest approached. In one sense it was just a job of filling up the bowls, but I became really interested in it. I went to the workshop where the gums arrived, saw the mixing, the blending that went in to create the grains that would in turn create the sweet-smelling odour before Zoroaster.

I loved the smell of frankincense above all the other smells. If it was up to me, I would have used that pure smell, but the skilled incense blenders knew better than I what would serve God best. So I kept my views to myself.

As the years have gone on, I have moved from filling the bowls to offering the incense. I sit now with the other priests, studying, watching, offering. It is a life of huge privilege, regular, predictable, holy.

So I was amazed when the unpredictable broke into the routine of my life. A new star arose in the night sky. A star that looked as though it might be leading us somewhere. It disturbed my routine to the extent that I decided to follow it. From living a life of such stability, predictability, from such a young age, I was disturbed out of my place and prepared for a journey. And don't ask me why, but among everything I took there was a box of pure frankincense, just the way I like it.

> God,
> disturb me out of my routine
> with the reality of your presence.
> Amen.

5 January

John 1.43–end

The next day Jesus decided to go to Galilee. He found Philip and said to him, 'Follow me.' Now Philip was from Bethsaida, the city of Andrew and Peter. Philip found Nathanael and said to him, 'We have found him about whom Moses in the law and also the prophets wrote, Jesus son of Joseph from Nazareth.' Nathanael said to him, 'Can anything good come out of Nazareth?' Philip said to him, 'Come and see.' When Jesus saw Nathanael coming towards him, he said of him, 'Here is truly an Israelite in whom there is no deceit!' Nathanael asked him, 'Where did you come to know me?' Jesus answered, 'I saw you under the fig tree before Philip

called you.' Nathanael replied, 'Rabbi, you are the Son
of God! You are the King of Israel!' Jesus answered, 'Do
you believe because I told you that I saw you under the
fig tree? You will see greater things than these.' And he
said to him, 'Very truly, I tell you, you will see heaven
opened and the angels of God ascending and descending
upon the Son of Man.'

It wasn't as simple as some coming from the north and
some from the south – this isn't an example of the old
north–south divide which can affect many places, not
just the UK. Philip, Andrew and Peter were from Galilee.
Nazareth is in another part of Galilee. It wasn't that Jesus
spoke with a different accent from them, they were all
northerners. But they were still prejudiced. Nathanael
assumed that nothing good or interesting could emerge
from a place like Nazareth, and especially not a Messiah.
The towns and villages around the Sea of Galilee, of which
Bethsaida was one, places like Capernaum and Tiberias,
places like Magdala, were busy and economically sound,
places of business and trading. What was the use of a
place like Nazareth?

I like to think of myself as not being prejudiced. I'm middle
class, moderately well educated, travelled, read. I vote
what I think is the right way. I preach an inclusive gospel
and try to live that out to the best of my ability. But scratch
me, and not so very deep, and I think you would find some
prejudice, some ways of judging people or places that I'm
not very proud of, some ways of categorizing people as
soon as I meet them that I feel ashamed to admit to.

Is it the newspaper I see someone reading? Is it when I
see a family emerging from a fast-food outlet? Is it when

I hear a particular regional accent that I can't bear? Is it hearing which programmes people watch? I was brought up to be a *Blue Peter* child; we never watched *Magpie* – that was a bit downmarket, all those dungarees and perms that John and Peter and Val would never have been seen in on screen!

Be honest. If you're not, you will never challenge those unworthy attitudes that are deep within you. And the bigger prejudices based on ethnicity, colour, gender, sexuality, wealth, education: have you really tackled those, as an individual, in the place where you work, in your church? I'm staggered to hear some of things that are said within the church when we are talking about women or gay people. It's more than shocking, it's scandalous – yet these are people who claim, like me, to be good Christians.

Philip tackles it head on. 'Come and see,' he says to Nathanael, and he takes him to Jesus.

We're not told if Nathanael leapt at the opportunity – 'Great, lead me to him!' – or whether he was more reluctant, had to be persuaded to have his opinions challenged and changed. The next thing we are actually told is that he is meeting Jesus, who shatters his preconceptions and leads to a moment of epiphany, a recognition that the one he had just dismissed is the one for whom he has been waiting and looking.

Could anything good come out of Nazareth? Of course Nathanael was wrong. Perhaps it wasn't the most obvious place in which to find anything amazing, life-changing, earth-shattering. But in fact it is the place in which God found Mary, the place in which God found Joseph. They were ordinary, unassuming people, the sort you might walk past and easily decide were nothing to bother with. But God found something there in Nazareth, something good that he couldn't find elsewhere: he found such deep faith, such obedient response, an open door through which his work of redemption could begin.

We have been Bethlehem bound. When we arrived in Bethlehem we could have walked past the stable door. It isn't the kind of place you would expect to find the Son of God; we could have ignored the signs and relied upon our own instincts, listened to our own prejudice – 'no way, not here, there must be a mistake, we'll look elsewhere'. But, thank God, we didn't. We stopped at that stable door and lifted the latch and went in and found God.

The only way in which we, individuals, institutions, communities, churches can confront the prejudice that lies just below the surface but manifests itself in so much of our lives and decision making is to hear Philip's invitation to us, day in, day out – 'Come and see'. It will be uncomfortable, talking to that homeless person, meeting the benefit claimant, working with refugees, worshipping in a different way, talking it through with a gay person, trying to understand the political stance so different from our own. But unless we are willing to do what Nathanael was willing to do, to go and see and to have his opinions confronted, challenged, changed, then we will never really meet God who is never the God we expect.

I love the poem 'Crabbit old woman'. It was written in 1966 by Phyllis McCormack while she was working in a nursing home, and it captures so well the judgemental attitudes that we can all have. It begins:

What do you see, what do you see?
Are you thinking, when you look at me –
A crabbit old woman, not very wise,
Uncertain of habit, with far-away eyes,
Who dribbles her food and makes no reply
When you say in a loud voice,
I do wish you'd try.

And it concludes:

So open your eyes, nurse, open and see,
Not a crabbit old woman, look closer –
See Me.[23]

Society, our lives, can only change and become more God-like if, on the journey we are making, we hear the invitation 'Come and see' – and respond.

Lord,
open my eyes to the truth around me;
cleanse my mind of old prejudice and judgements;
confront, challenge and change me.
Amen.

And now meet ... Balthazar

What are you looking at? Are you surprised that I'm black? Oh, don't look away now as though you've been caught out. I've become used to it. I stand out in the crowd, in the temple, among the Magi. But that is just the way it is. The world is bigger than your world. Get over it.

I'm sorry to react like that but occasionally it gets to me and at the moment I feel a bit unsettled, so I admit, I'm a bit jumpy. What am I doing here? Well, I could ask the same of you. I'm here because this is where I live, this is where I ended up when my family took to the road to escape the hunger where we were living. There had been no rain for ages, the crops had failed, the animals had left the watering holes because there was no longer any water. In the end my father decided we too had to go.

He was an apothecary and so he relied on the plants and the animals around us for the things that he needed to concoct. He was always in his workshop, perfecting an ointment, mixing an oil, a tincture for someone who had come to our door. 'Please, my child, make her well.' 'Help me with this sore, you must have a poultice.' 'I need to lay my wife to rest. Please sell me what I need.' The requests came day and night and my father always responded, a little phial here, a bundle there. And I learned a lot, assisting him, running for him.

When we settled here he continued his trade, his profession, and people forgot he was black and came to our door as they had done before. We learned new ways, ate new foods, worshipped new gods, or at least the old gods that were at the heart of the community that we now called home. When my father died I took over the business for a time but gradually I was drawn more to the temple, to the priesthood, for the healing and goodness that comes through faith; I became a Magus. Surprising, isn't it?

Of course, I brought my knowledge with me, and people still come to me with their living and their dead.

Last night I heard some of the others talking. They had seen a new star. Two of them were loading their camels to follow it. They were curious and so was I. Old Melchior was the first to spot it, young Caspar saw it as well. I made my way to the temple court. Caspar had caught up with Melchior and the two had decided to travel together.

'Can I join you?' I asked.

'You know what they say, "Two's company..."' responded Caspar.

But Melchior stopped him. 'We will need you,' he said to me. 'Bring your medicines, bring your ointments. We don't know where we are going; we don't know what we will need.'

So that is why I am here, with my bags and the tools of the apothecary – and I even brought myrrh, just in case.

> Loving God,
> heal my wounds
> and give me your peace.
> Amen.

6 January

Matthew 2.1–12

*In the time of King Herod, after Jesus was born in
Bethlehem of Judea, wise men from the East came to
Jerusalem, asking, 'Where is the child who has been
born king of the Jews? For we observed his star at its
rising, and have come to pay him homage.' When King
Herod heard this, he was frightened, and all Jerusalem
with him; and calling together all the chief priests and
scribes of the people, he inquired of them where the
Messiah was to be born. They told him, 'In Bethlehem
of Judea; for so it has been written by the prophet:
"And you, Bethlehem, in the land of Judah,
    are by no means least among the rulers of Judah;*

*for from you shall come a ruler
who is to shepherd my people Israel."'*

*Then Herod secretly called for the wise men and learned
from them the exact time when the star had appeared.
Then he sent them to Bethlehem, saying, 'Go and search
diligently for the child; and when you have found him,
bring me word so that I may also go and pay him
homage.' When they had heard the king, they set out;
and there, ahead of them, went the star that they had
seen at its rising, until it stopped over the place where
the child was. When they saw that the star had stopped,
they were overwhelmed with joy. On entering the house,
they saw the child with Mary his mother; and they
knelt down and paid him homage. Then, opening their
treasure-chests, they offered him gifts of gold, frankincense, and myrrh. And having been warned in a dream
not to return to Herod, they left for their own country
by another road.*

We began this journey, Bethlehem bound, recalling the
poem by T. S. Eliot 'The Journey of the Magi' and the way
in which he reflects on what Bishop Lancelot Andrewes
said in a sermon preached to the Court at Whitehall in
1622:

*A cold coming they had of it at this time of the year, just
the worst time of the year to take a journey, and specially
a long journey.*[24]

Today, the Feast of the Epiphany, is when we celebrate
their arrival, these visitors from the east with their strange
ways and significant gifts. The truth is of course that they
were not kings – well, not as far as scripture records –

and there is nowhere that says there were just the three of them. The three comes simply from the three gifts that they presented. But what we do know is that they had come on a long journey to be at this place. They were astronomers, probably, priests of another religion. Certainly they studied the stars for wisdom, and it was in the stars that they saw the sign which told them that the King of the Jews had been born.

It is the twelfth day of Christmas, but I imagine that time has moved on much more for the Holy Family. Our cribs do us a disservice. We bring in the figures of the 'kings' and put into the background the shepherd boy with his sheep and the older shepherd standing with his pipe, and the sheep and the ox and the hay are still all there. But the reading from Matthew mentions nothing about a stable. The stable is all in the Lucan account. As so often when we use the Bible in church we mix the stories up to create a helpful narrative and chronology and to give painters and producers of Christmas cards good but inaccurate images from which to work.

Matthew writes of their arrival at a house:

> On entering the house, they saw the child with Mary his mother. (Matthew 2.11)

Eliot also imagines what the Magi find on arrival following their long and difficult journey. His poem is crammed full of imagery that resonates with so much that will happen in the Gospels: three trees on the skyline, a hint of Calvary; a vine over the lintel, the precious blood of Christ in the eucharistic cup and maybe a pointer to the exodus and the marking of the lintels in the blood of the Lamb;

dice, suggesting the soldiers casting lots for Jesus' clothes at the foot of the cross; and empty wine skins, kicked away in preference for new skins that will hold the new wine of the kingdom.

There is more besides, I'm sure. But all Eliot says of the place where the Magi found Jesus was that they found it and that it was 'satisfactory'. I love that word in this line, it is slightly shocking. We would have thought it was all more than 'satisfactory'. But perhaps this has something to do with that ordinariness in the scene that we have noticed throughout this Christmas journey.

So, not a stable but a house. The family have moved out of temporary, unsatisfactory lodging into something satisfactory. There is a lovely poem by Frances Chesterton, which has been set to music by Howells and others, that tells of the arrival of the Magi at their journey's end. It's entitled 'Here is the little door'.

Here is the little door,
lift up the latch, oh lift!
We need not wander more,
but enter with our gift;
Our gift of finest gold.
Gold that was never bought or sold;
Myrrh to be strewn about his bed;
Incense in clouds about His head;
All for the child that stirs not in His sleep,
But holy slumber holds with ass and sheep.

Bend low about His bed,
For each He has a gift;
See how His eyes awake,

Lift up your hands, O lift!
For gold, He gives a keen-edged sword.
(Defend with it thy little Lord!)
For incense, smoke of battle red,
Myrrh for the honoured happy dead;
Gifts for His children, terrible and sweet;
Touched by such tiny hands,
and Oh such tiny feet.[25]

Chesterton suggests that the child gave back to his children gifts that mirror those they bring. It is a lovely idea, and there at the end is the hint at the Passion with the reference to the tiny hands and tiny feet which, when a man's, will bear the marks of nails and become the signs of love.

But at the beginning of the poem, she writes: 'lift up the latch, oh lift!'

I wonder whether, when she was writing this, she had in mind one of the most famous pictures of the Pre-Raphaelite era, *The Light of the World* by Holman Hunt. The two most famous 'originals' hang in the stunning setting of Keble College Chapel in Oxford and the equally stunning St Paul's Cathedral. The image is well known, and one of the most important details is that there is no latch on the outside. Jesus knocks at the little door but has to be let in; we lift the latch. The Magi found the door and lifted the latch and entered the house and found the one for whom they had been searching, the one for whom they had been Bethlehem bound.

Jesus will never force himself into your life, he just isn't like that. He leaves us in control, to welcome him into our lives, to enter his house, or to stay away and keep him out. It was the last act of the journey for the Magi, to lift the latch and enter the house and find the child and his mother, to worship and adore. When they had adored him and given their gifts they left by another road. They couldn't travel the same road again; life for them had been transformed, changed. Eliot in his poem speaks of the old dispensation to which they could never return with comfort.

Towards the end of the final book in the Bible, the book of the Revelation to St John, the 'Evangelist of the Incarnation', we find these words:

> 'The first things have passed away ... See, I am making all things new.' (Revelation 21.4, 5)

For the Magi and for us all things are new. The old dispensation is no more, there is a new covenant and a new world and we have found it in Bethlehem. But unlike the Magi you have no need to head off, to hurry away. We can stay in the house and linger, for Christmas carries on. And Christmas always carries on, for 'the Word was made flesh and lived among us', and that was true then and it remains true now.

Creator of the heavens,
who led the Magi by a star
to worship the Christ-child:
guide and sustain us,
that we may find our journey's end
in Jesus Christ our Lord.
Amen.[26]

And now meet ... the Wise Men

Melchior says:

We didn't arrive a moment too soon. My old bones couldn't take any more, even the cushions that surrounded me as we rode the camels couldn't stop the aches and pains. And then there was Herod. I had heard of him of course and we needed to see him. The more I studied the star on the way the more I knew that it was heralding the birth of a new king. As we got closer we began to talk about what we would do when we got there. The polite thing and the right thing would be to pay our respects to the king and, after all, if a new king was to be born it must be in the palace. Although the voice of my wife was in my ear, urging me to go nowhere near Herod. But we had no choice – we were strangers in the land. And so as we got closer we decided to go first to Jerusalem, and in truth that was where the star was heading.

As the eldest I had to do the talking, explain the journey. And he was interested, very interested. His own priests shared their knowledge with us, from their scriptures. But when we were ready to leave the king said to us, 'When you have found him, bring me word so that I may also go and pay him homage.'

To be polite I said, 'Of course.' But I wasn't sure. There was something about him I just didn't trust.

Caspar says:

We were glad to leave Jerusalem. Not that it isn't impressive. We saw their temple, gleaming, gold and white marble, visible from a distance, the glow of the fires from the altars of offering. This wasn't the backwater I was led to expect. Herod's palace was amazing, but none of us felt comfortable. So, with the directions in our head and the star before us, we left the city and headed into the countryside. It wasn't far at all; a little town, nestling in the hills, sheep grazing, barley growing.

We didn't have to worry about finding the right house. The star did the work for us and it stopped right over the place to where we had been bound, drawn by the light.

Balthazar says:

We got down from our camels and straightened our robes. Each of us held a gift, for a king. But we were at no palace, just a little door with a latch. One of us, I honestly can't remember who, lifted it and we went in.

Melchior says:

And I gave him my gold.

Caspar says:

And I gave him my frankincense.

Balthazar says:

And I gave him my myrrh and we worshipped.

> What can I give Him, poor as I am?
> If I were a shepherd, I would bring a lamb;
> If I were a Wise Man, I would do my part;
> Yet what I can I give Him: give my heart.[27]

2 February

Candlemas, Jerusalem Bound

8.00am

Luke 2.22–24

> When the time came for their purification according to
> the law of Moses, they brought him up to Jerusalem to
> present him to the Lord (as it is written in the law of the
> Lord, 'Every firstborn male shall be designated as holy
> to the Lord'), and they offered a sacrifice according to
> what is stated in the law of the Lord, 'a pair of turtle-
> doves or two young pigeons'.

The dawn is breaking, and people are setting off on journeys. The shepherds have been in the fields all night, the

innkeepers are looking after their guests, bread is being baked and in the yards donkeys are getting ready for a hard day's work. People are setting off on journeys. An old man leaves his home, he's Jerusalem bound. It's a journey he makes regularly, from his home to the temple at the heart of the city. In the precincts of the temple an old woman is stirring. She never leaves the temple. She never travels, she is where she belongs.

In Bethlehem a young family are getting ready to leave their home. Its 40 days since the young woman, the young girl, gave birth to a baby boy. She and her husband are not from these parts – well, not now. Joseph's family originated from here, but he moved a long time ago, from Judea to Galilee, and it was the Roman occupation that had brought him back. They had called for a census, and everyone had to go back to their place of origin. So at the very worst time, Mary about to give birth, in the worst season of the year, they were Bethlehem bound.

Those 40 days after the birth of their baby had been like no others in their lives. People they did not know had come to see them and they talked of their child in such strange ways, with words that they couldn't get out of their minds. Mary was forever going back over what people had said as they saw their child, as they saw Jesus.

Now, on this cold morning, in the dawn light, they left their house. Mary rode on the donkey again, the one that had brought them to Bethlehem, and they set off to Jerusalem. Last time the baby was in her womb, this time her son is in her arms. They too were Jerusalem bound.

But it was not the Roman occupying force that was demanding the journey, but their own law. They were making this journey to fulfil the demands of the law, God's law, which asked that, in thanksgiving for the birth of their first son, an offering was made. It was a life for a life, an offering of a bird for the life of the child. A life for a life. They would buy their offering when they got to Jerusalem, buy from those who sold in the temple courts, make an offering of love, for love, of life, for life. Now there was a journey ahead of them.

And as the dawn breaks we are setting off on a journey, to work, to school, to the shops, to family, to friends, a journey of remembering as we sit, a physical journey, a mental one. And in the morning we too prepare to make an offering, not of a life but of our life, an offering in thanksgiving to God for this new day, this fortieth day, with all that it holds in store for us, an offering of love for love.

> Lord,
> as the dawn breaks
> as the day begins
> accept our praise
> accept our thanks
> that we may walk this day
> with you.
> Amen.

10.00am

Luke 2.25–35

> *Now there was a man in Jerusalem whose name was*
> *Simeon; this man was righteous and devout, looking*
> *forward to the consolation of Israel, and the Holy Spirit*
> *rested on him. It had been revealed to him by the Holy*
> *Spirit that he would not see death before he had seen the*
> *Lord's Messiah. Guided by the Spirit, Simeon came into*
> *the temple; and when the parents brought in the child*
> *Jesus, to do for him what was customary under the law,*
> *Simeon took him in his arms and praised God, saying,*
> > *'Master, now you are dismissing your servant in peace,*
> > > *according to your word;*
> > *for my eyes have seen your salvation,*
> > > *which you have prepared in the presence of*
> > > *all peoples,*
> > *a light for revelation to the Gentiles*
> > > *and for glory to your people Israel.'*
> *And the child's father and mother were amazed at what*
> *was being said about him. Then Simeon blessed them*
> *and said to his mother Mary, 'This child is destined for*
> *the falling and the rising of many in Israel, and to be a*
> *sign that will be opposed so that the inner thoughts of*
> *many will be revealed—and a sword will pierce your*
> *own soul too.'*

He was like a bird, old Simeon, always alert, always on the
lookout, missing nothing, watching, 'eyes in the back of

his head' they said. He was known by everyone; he'd been around so long and as he approached the temple no one was surprised to see him. Taking in everything that was already happening, looking at who was there, he made his way through the courts. The traders were there with their turtle doves and pigeons, the tables of the money changers had been set out, the rate of exchange was being negotiated – just how much could they get out of the pilgrims that day?

Simeon carried on through this noisy, bustling scene, to a place where he always stopped, from where he could wait and watch. T. S. Eliot reflects in his poem 'A Song for Simeon' on the man he describes as keeping 'faith and fast', his life 'like a feather on the back of my hand'. His words seem to echo what the great Hildegard of Bingen wrote of her own life as being 'a feather on the breath of God'. There is a gentle, timeless, calm waiting going on.

Mary and Joseph arrive with their baby. It hasn't been a long journey, though uphill, from Bethlehem to Jerusalem. It was an amazing sight when they first saw the temple gleaming in the winter light, and the people moving up and down the steps that led into the courts and ultimately to the heart of this sacred place, the Holy of Holies – but they wouldn't be going there.

They left the donkey, for their return journey, and made their way in. First they had to change the money they had with them into the money they could use in the temple. Then they had to find the person who sold the pigeons. Mary was comforting her child while Joseph did the deals with the money changers, the animal traders, slick city people who knew how things worked while they, from out of town, were 'rednecks', lacking in city sophistication. The traders could see them coming.

The transactions done, they entered further into the temple to make the offering and to present their child to God. From the brightness outside they were struck by the gloom inside, until their eyes got used to it and then they could make out the priests going about their business, those on the rota for that day, men like Mary's cousin's husband, Zechariah, who had been struck dumb in this very place.

And the old man, the bird-like man, watching from the sidelines, steps out of the gloom into the half light of the place and takes their baby from them and sings of the light that has come into the world.

Once again they are amazed. Angels, shepherds, strangers, and now this old man, all had said such wonderful things about their child, about Jesus, words of hope and joy, words of God and things made new, words of peace, words of comfort.

But then the man, Simeon, turns to Mary and his words are as harsh as the cold winds that had accompanied them as they were Jerusalem bound in the early light of day – 'and a sword will pierce your own soul too'.

There is a bittersweet feeling to this day. It is the conclusion of the Christmas season, and we can pack the cribs away and take down the final decorations. This is the day of the last vestiges of Christmas, but in a strange way it is the first day of Passion. Sometimes in the Candlemas liturgy the clergy will change from white vestments to end with purple ones, and the texts for the ending of the

Eucharist reinforce this change of mood. The procession has moved from the altar to the font and the priest says:

> *We stand near the place of new birth.*
> *Let us shine with the light of your love.*
> *We turn from the crib to the cross.*
> *Let us shine with the light of your love.*[28]

'We turn from the crib to the cross.' As the famous Latin antiphon dating from the eighth century says:

> *Media vita in morte sumus.*

'In the midst of life we are in death.' It is the bittersweet truth of this wonderful feast. Mary feels it as she holds her child, as she will feel it in not so many years when she will hold her child again as he is taken lifeless from the cross and laid in her arms. Mary could not escape it and Simeon, who had seen it all, does not spare her from the truth. And I wish it were not so and I am sorry to ruin this last day of Christmas. But grown-up religion can cope with the truth. If Mary couldn't escape it, why should I? If a sword should pierce her soul, why not mine? To expect it to be otherwise is to live in a fool's paradise. But the 'Cheshire Cat' grin that some Christians display suggests that they cannot really accept that, while we believe with Julian of Norwich that 'All shall be well, and all shall be well and all manner of thing shall be well'; the truth is that life can be hard, and that faith and hope and love are not a means of escape from reality but a means of encounter with it. This is the mature faith that this powerful encounter between the old man waiting for death and the young girl holding new life in her arms embodies within the life of the church.

In some years the Feast of the Annunciation and the celebration of Good Friday fall on the same day. John Donne writes about this beautifully in his poem 'The Annunciation and Passion', in which he says this of Mary and the bittersweet experience which we share with her:

She sees at once the Virgin Mother stay
Reclused at home, public at Golgotha;
Sad and rejoiced she's seen at once, and seen
At almost fifty, and at scarce fifteen;
At once a son is promised her, and gone;
Gabriell gives Christ to her, He her to John;
Not fully a mother, she's in orbity;
At once receiver and the legacy.[29]

That sweet and bitter taste that life leaves in the mouth;
Lord, may those tasting it today,
know strength and faith in you.
Amen.

12 noon

Luke 2.36–38

There was also a prophet, Anna the daughter of Phanuel, of the tribe of Asher. She was of a great age, having lived with her husband for seven years after her marriage, then as a widow to the age of eighty-four. She never left the temple but worshipped there with fasting and prayer night and day. At that moment she came, and began to praise God and to speak about the child to all who were looking for the redemption of Jerusalem.

Someone had been there all the time. Anna is a fantastic character, this prophet who lived in the temple, this widow for most of her life, living a consecrated life with God. We have, of course, met her already on this journey. She is one of those, like Simeon, who steps on to the stage of the Gospels just for a moment and then fades back into the shadows. But she is also one of those who brings someone else with them.

When Mark tells us about Simon of Cyrene on the way of the cross, he just mentions that he is the father of Alexander and Rufus – as though we should know who they were – perhaps because his original readers did know who they were and thought 'oh, them', 'oh, him'. In a similar way Luke mentions that Anna is the daughter of Phanuel. From our former meeting with her we understand something of what this means. But that name, fixing her in history, fixing her in a family and a line, also does something else.

This is the only mention we get of Phanuel, but the interesting thing is what his name means. Any Hebrew name ending in –el has some reference to God and this name is no exception. As we now know the name means 'Face of God'. When I learned that I was thrilled. It's just an incidental, almost throwaway part of the story, but there in that name is something so significant for this final act of the Christmas narrative. There is nothing spare or throwaway in the scriptures!

Why were we Bethlehem bound? We made the journey to see the face of God in the child in the crib, just as we will be Jerusalem bound in just a few weeks' time and will see the face of God in Jesus on the cross. The feast we celebrate today, the Presentation of Christ in the Temple, is another moment of epiphany, of seeing who Jesus is, and in Simeon's song so much of this is expressed.

Jesus is the one for whom we have been waiting; Jesus is the light that will lighten all people; Jesus is, in the words of the writer of the Letter to the Hebrews,

> *The reflection of God's glory and the exact imprint of God's very being.* (Hebrews 1.3)

Jesus is the face of God.

That reading from the Letter to the Hebrews takes us back to Christmas morning when we looked for the first time into the crib and saw the face of Jesus and saw the face of God; and as Anna speaks of the child she does so as the daughter of the one whose name was 'Face of God'.

In the musical *Les Misérables* the final song ends with these amazing words: 'To love another person is to see the face of God.' It is a powerful truth with which to bring a powerful musical to a conclusion. Today, we too look for the face of God in the faces around us.

Lord Jesus, may I see your face,
God's face,
in the faces around me.
Amen.

4.00pm

Luke 2.39–40

> *When they had finished everything required by the law of the Lord, they returned to Galilee, to their own town of Nazareth. The child grew and became strong, filled with wisdom; and the favour of God was upon him.*

What a journey! When we set out we were simply following the angels' song and look where it took us, to a stable and a birth and such joy as the world has never known. For Mary and Joseph, with their child, the time had come to move, to leave Bethlehem behind. The law had been fulfilled and now they had to get back to their life, their ordinary life. But Mary held something extraordinary in her arms, a child with the favour of God upon him.

St Matthew's Gospel records a brief period of exile, as refugees in Egypt, escaping Herod's wrath. But when the coast was clear, and following the angel's instruction, they headed back. The carpenter's shop would be waiting for them, there was business to pick up, water would need to be drawn from the well, their friends and neighbours in their synagogue would be waiting for them. And what would Mary say about what had taken place? We don't know because, apart from an incident when Jesus was 12 and the family had come back to Jerusalem and the temple for his Bar Mitzva, the next 30 years are lived for Jesus and his family in obscurity, an ordinary life, like most of our ordinary lives.

But for us in the church calendar time moves much more quickly: very soon it will be Ash Wednesday and another journey will take place.

Ralph Vaughan Williams, the great English composer of the twentieth century, was also a collector of English folk songs and carols and helped to introduce many of them back into the choral and church repertoire. One of my favourite but lesser-known carols takes us on the journey we have just completed and beyond. For in this trad-itional carol, which originates in Derbyshire, the journey of the Christian life is seamless and 'sweet Jesus' is there as our companion throughout. Travel well and with God's blessing.

It was on Christmas day,
And all in the morning,
Our Saviour was born,
And our Heavenly King;
And was not this a joyful thing,
And sweet Jesus they called Him by name.

It was on New Year's Day
And all in the morning,
They circumcised our Saviour
And our Heavenly King;
And was not this a joyful thing,
And sweet Jesus they called Him by name.

It was on Twelfth Day
And all in the morning,

The Wise Men were led
To our Heavenly King;
And was not this a joyful thing,
And sweet Jesus they called Him by name.

It was on Twentieth Day
And all in the morning,
The Wise Men returned
From our Heavenly King;
And was not this a joyful thing,
And sweet Jesus they called Him by name.

It was on Candlemas Day
And all in the morning,
They visited the Temple
With our Heavenly King;
And was not this a joyful thing,
And sweet Jesus they called Him by name.

It was on Holy Wednesday
And all in the morning,
That Judas Betrayed
Our dear Heavenly King;
And was not this a joyful thing,
And sweet Jesus they called Him by name.

It was on Sheer Thursday
And all in the morning,
They plaited a crown of thorns,
For our Heavenly King;
And was not this a joyful thing,
And sweet Jesus they called Him by name.

It was on Good Friday
And all in the morning,
They crucified our Saviour
And our Heavenly King;
And was not this a joyful thing,
And sweet Jesus they called Him by name.

It was on Easter Day
And all in the morning,
Our Saviour arose
Our own Heavenly King;
They sun and the moon
They did both rise with Him
And sweet Jesus we'll call Him by name.[30]

Notes and Acknowledgements

Where prayers are not attributed they are the work of the author.

Unless otherwise indicated, all biblical quotations are from the NRSV Anglicized Edition, copyright © 1989, 1995, National Council of the Churches of Christ in the United States of America. Used by permission. All rights reserved worldwide.

1 The Bidding Prayer is available at: www.kings.cam.ac.uk/sites/default/files/documents//9lc-order-service-2018.pdf (accessed 10.2.20).
2 Antiphon, *Common Worship: Daily Prayer*, London: Church House Publishing, 2011, p. 211.
3 Lancelot Andrewes, 'Sermons of the Nativity, Preached upon Christmas Day', preached before King James at Whitehall on 25 December 1622.
4 C. G. Jung, *Memories, Dreams, Reflections*, London: Collins, Routledge and Kegan Paul, 1963.
5 Protoevangelium of James, available at: www.newadvent.org/fathers/0847.htm (accessed 11.2.22).
6 Sister Joyce Yarrow CSF, *The Daily Office SSF*, London: Bloomsbury Continuum, 2021.
7 Joy Cowley, 'A Modern Magnificat (The Song of Mary)', Gecko Press, permission applied for.
8 St Ambrose, *Commentary of Saint Ambrose on the Gospel According to Saint Luke*, trans. Íde M. Ní Riain, London: Halcyon Press, 2001.
9 Chief Rabbi Lord Sacks, 'Celebrating Faith, Altruism and Our Modern Community', 5 July 2011, available at: www.huffpost.com/entry/religion-community_b_890357 (accessed 11.2.22).

10 Antoine de Saint-Exupéry, *Night Flight*, London: Penguin Books, 1939.
11 Jean Paul Sartre, *The Devil and the Good Lord*, New York: Alfred A. Knopf, 1960, Act 1.
12 Joseph Mohr, 1818, trans. John Freeman Young, 1859.
13 *Common Worship: Services and Prayers for the Church of England*, London: Church House Publishing, 2000.
14 Alister McGrath, *The Journey: A Pilgrim in the Lands of the Spirit*, London: Hodder & Stoughton, 1999.
15 *Common Worship: Services and Prayers.*
16 Christina Rossetti, 'Love Came Down at Christmas', 1885.
17 *Common Worship: Daily Prayer*, p. 525.
18 Evelyn Underhill, *The Spiritual Life*, Harrisburg PA: Morehouse Publishing, 1937.
19 Traditional prayer, often known as the Jesus Prayer.
20 *Common Worship: Collects and Post Communions in Contemporary Language*, London: Church House Publishing, 2021.
21 Adapted from penitential material, *Common Worship: New Patterns for Worship*, London: Church House Publishing, 2002, p. 97.
22 William Blake, 'The Lamb', 1789.
23 Phyllis McCormack, 'Crabbit old woman', published in *Nursing Mirror*, 1972.
24 Lancelot Andrewes, 'Sermons of the Nativity'.
25 Frances Chesterton, 'Here is the little door', 1918.
26 *Common Worship: Additional Collects*, London: Church House Publishing, 2017.
27 Christina Rossetti, 'In the Bleak Mid-winter', 1872.
28 *Common Worship: Times and Seasons*, London: Church House Publishing, 2013.
29 John Donne, 'The Annunciation and Passion', 1608.
30 'It was on Christmas day', traditional carol collected by Ralph Vaughan Williams. His arrangement is published by Stainer & Bell.

Acknowledgements of Illustrations

Beginning the Journey: Mary and Joseph on the Way to Bethlehem, Hugo van der Goes, Uffizi Gallery, Florence, https://commons.wikimedia.org/.

17 December: Detail of Jesse Tree from St Mary's, Shrewsbury, https://commons.wikimedia.org/, CCT Digital.

18 December: Dream of St Joseph, http://www.blessedjoseph. blogspot.com.

19 December: Zechariah, Elizabeth and John, https://www.flickr. com/photos/pelegrino, Nick Johnson.

20 December: The Annunciation of Mary, Fra Angelico, Museum of San Marco, Florence, https://commons.wikimedia.org/, Carulmare.

21 December: The Visitation, Domenico Ghirlandaio, https://commons.wikimedia.org/, Sailko.

22 December: The Madonna of the Magnificat, Botticelli, Uffizi Gallery, Florence, https://commons.wikimedia.org/, ZgEiSSEEoWAUdw.

23 December: Zechariah Naming John the Baptist, Church of St Edward the Martyr, Castle Donington, Leicestershire, https://commons.wikimedia.org/, Aidan McRae Thomson.

24 December: John the Baptist with the Lamb, Circle of Sisto Badalocchio, https://commons.wikimedia.org/.

24 December: Mary and Joseph Looking for an Inn, https://www. spiritualdirection.com/2017/12/20/the-journey-to-bethlehem.

25 December: The Nativity of Jesus, https://www.istockphoto. com.

26 December: St Stephen, https://www.ststephenthemartyrsc.ca/ new-to-st-stephens/st-stephen-the-martyr.

27 December: St John writing the Book of Revelation, https://www.istockphoto.com.

28 December: Joseph's Dream and the Flight into Egypt, Cappella Palatina, Palermo, https://www.christianiconography. info.

29 December: The Death of St Thomas Becket, https://www. historic-uk.com/HistoryUK/HistoryofEngland/Thomas-Becket.

30 December: Anna the Prophetess, http://www.women inthebible.net/women-bible-old-new-testaments/anna.

31 December: Figure of Christ, Heinrich Hofmann, https://commons.wikimedia.org/.

1 January: Annunciation of the Shepherds, Taddeo Gaddi, Baroncelli Chapel, Church of Santa Croce, Florence, https://commons.wikimedia.org/.

2 January: St John the Baptist, https://www.istockphoto.com.

3 January: Jesus Baptized by John, https://www.scriptoriumdaily. com/the-baptism-of-christ-2-john-the-baptist.

4 January: Christ Pantocrator, Cappella Palatine Chapel, Palazzo Reale, Palermo, Sicily, https://commons.wikimedia.org/, José Luiz Bernardes Ribeiro.

5 January: Philip meets Nathanael Beside a Fig Tree, Chartres Cathedral, https://commons.wikimedia.org/.

6 January: Adoration of the Magi, Gentile da Fabriano, Uffizi Gallery, Florence, https://wikioo.org/en/paintings.php?refarticle= 5ZKCEU/.

Jerusalem Bound: Adoration of the Magi, Gentile da Fabriano, Uffizi, Florence, https://.en.wikipedia.org.